30 DAYS TO
RUTH/ESTHER

PORTRAITS OF PROVIDENCE

Lyla Curtis
Ps. 138:8

30 Days to Ruth/Esther

Portraits of Providence

Lyla Curtis

Seed Publishing Group, LLC
Timmonsville, South Carolina

30 Days to Ruth/Esther: A Devotional Commentary

Copyright © 2018 by Lyla Curtis

Published by:
Seed Publishing Group
2570 Double C Farm Ln
Timmonsville, SC 29161
seed–publishing–group.com

Edited by:
Bill Curtis, Ph.D.
Dwayne Milioni, Ph.D.

All rights reserved. No part of this book may be reproduced or transmitted in any form or by any means, electronic or mechanical, including photocopying and recording, or by any information storage or retrieval system, except as may be expressly permitted in writing by the publisher. Requests for permission should be addressed in writing to Seed Publishing Group, LLC; 2570 Double C Farm Lane; Timmonsville, SC 29161.

Scripture quotations are from The Holy Bible, English Standard Version® (ESV®), copyright © 2001 by Crossway, a publishing ministry of Good News Publishers. Used by permission. All rights reserved.

To order additional copies of this resource visit
www.seed–publishing–group.com.

Library of Congress Control Number: 2017919320

ISBN–13: 978-0-9985451-2-7

Printed in the United States of America

Dedication

*To Bill — because you loved me...,
believed in me, and encouraged me
out of my comfort zone.*

Contents

Preface xi

Day 1   Portraits of Providence 1

Day 2   Introduction to Ruth 5

Day 3   Ruth 1:1—5 and 20—22 11

Day 4   Ruth 1:6—15 19

Day 5   Ruth 1:16—19 27

Day 6   Ruth 1:22—2:4 33

Day 7   Ruth 2:5—12 39

Day 8   Ruth 2:13—23 47

Day 9   Ruth 3:1—6 53

Day 10   Ruth 3:7—18 61

Day 11   Ruth 4:1—12 67

Day 12   Ruth 4:13—22 73

Day 13   Reflections on the Book of Ruth 79

Day 14   Introduction to Esther 85

Contents

Day 15	Esther 1:1—9	91
Day 16	Esther 1:10—22	97
Day 17	Esther 2	103
Day 18	Esther 2	111
Day 19	Esther 3:1—6	119
Day 20	Esther 3:7—15	125
Day 21	Esther 4	133
Day 22	Esther 5	141
Day 23	Esther 6	149
Day 24	Esther 7	155
Day 25	Esther 8	161
Day 26	Esther 9—10	167
Day 27	The Particulars of Providence	173
Day 28	Vessels of Providence	179
Day 29	Comfort or Courage?	185
Day 30	Life-Changing Encounters	191

Finding L.I.F.E. in Jesus! 195

Preface

Few books in the Bible elicit more interest or questions than the Books of Ruth and Esther. Located in the historical books of the Old Testament, they are the only books in the Bible that are named for women. These books depict dark days in the history of Israel. Written during the time of the judges, the Book of Ruth is the love story of King David's grandparents and explains how a Moabite woman ended up in the lineage of King Jesus. It is a book about love lost and love regained, and it provides a most excellent example of the beauty of God's redemptive work, both then and now.

Esther, on the other hand, is written during Israel's captivity in Persia. It recounts the near genocide of the Jewish people, and God's miraculous rescue though the efforts of the young Jewish queen, Esther. It is a spy-thriller—full of political intrigue, assassination attempts, and sexual debauchery. Interestingly, this book never mentions God's name at all. Yet, few books in all of Scripture provide a better picture of God's meticulous providence as he works out his sovereign will for his people and the world.

For the next 30 days, I will take you on an unforgettable journey through the lives of these two incredible women: Ruth and Esther. As a woman, I can connect deeply with their struggles. Each day, I will explore their unique stories, as they wrestled with fear and faith in the presence of loss, loneliness, and oppression. As I do, you will come

Preface

to understand Ruth and Esther's lack of power and control over their lives, and the danger they faced while living in an ancient, patriarchal society. Through it all, God will remind us, both women and men alike, that he works in our lives to accomplish his purpose, even when our situations seem impossible.

–Lyla Curtis

Day 1

Portraits Of Providence

There are many women whose stories are splashed throughout the histories of the inspired word of God: wicked divas, saintly darlings, and courageous heroines. However, there are only two women who have books of the Bible named specifically for them—Ruth and Esther. Consider how amazing it is that out of the 36 specific proper names used to title 40 books of the Bible, two of them are women. This makes them pretty special and worthy of close examination! For the next 30 days, we will study these two remarkable women.

Similarities and differences mark the comparison of Ruth and Esther. Ruth was a converted, pagan Gentile, while Esther was a true-blue, Jewish girl. Ruth's faith was evident in her daily faithfulness to God's guiding hand, while Esther's faith found its climax in a few courageous, life-threatening requests. Ruth's appeal was found in her sun-drenched skin, calloused hands, and hard work ethic, while Esther's natural beauty was enhanced by expensive skin treatments, exotic perfumes, and her modest demeanor. Both were guided by God-fearing mentors—Ruth by her mother-in-law, Naomi, and Esther by her cousin and father figure, Mordecai. Both knew what it felt like to experience heart-breaking losses which affected their characters and their futures. Most importantly, both Ruth

Out of the 36 specific proper names used to title 40 books of the Bible, two of them are women.

and Esther were greatly used by God to fulfill divine purposes.

Don't make the mistake of passing these books off as books for women only. Ruth and Esther may be the main, female characters, but there are other interesting characters in these dramas with whom we can all identify. Regardless of gender, marital status, or age, the books of Ruth and Esther have something valuable for everyone. Public official, business owner, employee, parent, child, in-law, friend, or family member—each one can relate to something or someone in these powerful stories. The history buff will recognize the significance of the events to the Jewish people. The literary scholar can enjoy the beauty of these well-written narratives. The racial and political intrigue in the Book of Esther will fascinate the mystery lover and conspiracy theorist. The hopeless romantic will delight in the romance stories so beautifully portrayed in both books. There may even be something for the fashionista and beauty expert. Undoubtedly, all worshipers of God will rejoice to see the unmistakable illustrations of the providential hand of God woven throughout both narratives, reminding us that God is in control and that his plan for redemption cannot be thwarted.

Both of these books paint beautiful portraits of Providence. A pastor friend calls it "Sovereignty in the Shadows." While these books are named for specific, historical figures, God is the main character in both books. The Book of Ruth mentions him openly, while the Book of Esther never mentions him at all. Nevertheless, God's hand moves the course of events in unmistakable ways throughout both books. His moves are both subtle and bold at the same time.

Both Ruth and Esther were greatly used by God to fulfill divine purposes.

Day 1

We can learn much about God's character traits from reading these two books. He is sovereign, but he chooses to use sinful creatures to fulfill his divine purposes. He is the personification of covenant love, yet he is the righteous defender of his people, exacting punishment on those who seek to destroy them. He permits adversity to fall on his people, but he uses it to accomplish his plans. He fulfills his redemptive plan through the nation and people he calls his own, yet he works specifically through the pagan nations and empires of the world, too.

These two books are narratives—written stories. The Bible is full of narratives, because God loves stories. Jesus loved stories, too. That's why he used parables, stories, and illustrative examples so often. We love stories, too. It stands to reason, because we are image-bearers of God. We relate to stories, because they allow us to identify with other people. We can learn from their successes and their failures. We will have the chance to do both as we look at Ruth and Esther's stories. But the most important lessons will come, not from observing their lives, but from seeing God at work and remembering that he is still at work today.

> *God is in control and his plan for redemption cannot be thwarted.*

Food for Thought — Contemplate what you currently know about Ruth and Esther. Maybe you are a Bible scholar that's done extensive research into these two characters. Maybe you remember these fascinating stories from Sunday School classes long ago. Or, maybe your knowledge only goes as far as the Veggie Tales version of Esther (If this is the case, hopefully you know that Esther really isn't a leek). Maybe you've watched the movie, "One Night with the King (2006 release)," and wondered how accurate it is. Why are you reading this devotional? What intrigues you about these books or these women?

Faith in Action — Find a journal or notebook to use as you journey through this study. Write down some observations you currently have about Ruth and Esther. Also, write down your expectations of what you hope to gain from reading this devotional. At the end of these 30 days, I will encourage you to look back and see what new truths you have gleaned from your study and what God desires to accomplish in your life using the lessons you learn.

Prayer — God in heaven, divine Author of Scripture, I ask you to guide me into all truth as I study these two books of the Bible for the next 30 days. Increase my knowledge of the significance of these narratives. Teach me more about who you are and your eternal purposes for the world and my life. Make clear to me your larger redemptive story as told through the events in these books of the Bible. Help me to embrace and apply your truths to my life. Open the eyes of my heart, Lord!

Introduction to Ruth

"The Book of Ruth has been called the most beautiful short story ever written (Expositors Bible Commentary, Vol. 3, Gaebelein, p. 509)." Most commentaries, books, or articles written about Ruth agree that it is a phenomenal piece of literature. Johann Wolfgang von Goethe, a great German literary figure of the modern era, reportedly labeled this piece of anonymous, yet unexcelled, literature as "the loveliest, complete work on a small scale." What Venus is to statuary and the Mona Lisa is to paintings, Ruth is to literature (The MacArthur Bible Commentary, p. 288). Jewish tradition says that Samuel is the author of this book, but there is no internal or external proof. The only thing about which scholars agree is that the author was a skilled, literary writer.

In Judaism, this Old Testament book is very significant. Throughout Jewish history, Ruth has been one of five books read at various Jewish festivals. These five books are called the Megilloth, meaning "five scrolls," and Rabbis read these books in the synagogue on special occasions. One of the occasions was the Feast of Weeks (also called Pentecost), which marked the end of grain harvest. With its portrayal of the harvest scenes in chapters 2 and 3, the Book of Ruth was an appropriate read during this feast.

Several themes run throughout the book. In *The Theology of the Book of Ruth,* Ronald M. Hals says, "With

God chooses the most unlikely people to accomplish his purposes in this world.

virtually his every word the author is endeavoring to present the providence of God (8)." He calls it "divine causality (77)." In other words, the events in this story were divinely *caused*. Two other theological ideas are redemption and reconciliation. There are 23 occurrences of the word *ga'al* in Ruth (EBC, 513). The Hebrew word *ga'al* or *go'el* means "kinsman redeemer" or "close relative." Ruth the Moabite, a non-Jew, illustrates that God's redemptive plan extends beyond the Jews to Gentiles. She also demonstrates that women are co-heirs with men of God's salvation grace (MBC, 289). Another theme pictured is true, selfless commitment in relationships and friendships. For all these reasons and more, the Book of Ruth stands out as a book worthy of our time and study.

For the next two weeks, let's set our calendars to meet daily over coffee with our first amazing woman, Ruth. Let's listen as she tells us her story. Of course, Naomi, her mother-in-law, will have to join us as well. Their stories are so intertwined that we cannot hear one without the other. Don't worry! Surprisingly, it will be much more pleasant than we might expect from the normal mother and daughter-in-law relationship. It will be fun to imagine "talking" with them and "listening" to their story. If we really could sit down with them, perhaps they would share a good barley cake recipe, reveal the secrets of how to be the boss everybody loves, give us advice about love and commitment, and tell us what muscles we'd use and how many calories we'd burn by gleaning wheat! But, one thing is for sure. As they tell us their story, we will hear the recurring theme of the providence of God as he protected them, taught them, guided their steps, and brought about something truly amazing in their lives; something they couldn't accomplish on their own.

First, we need to know a few things about our leading lady and her background. Five times in this short book

Day 2

she is referred to as "Ruth the Moabite." It's as if we need to be constantly reminded of who she was and where she had lived. However, the book gives no explanation of the country of Moab or the Moabite people. All we know is that Elimelech and his family moved to Moab, and his sons married women from Moab. We are left to research Moab on our own, and it's vital to our study. It will help us understand the enormity of God's providence and grace in Ruth's story.

The Moabites were a race of people born from the incestuous union between Lot and his oldest daughter, after they fled God's destruction of Sodom and Gomorrah (Gen 19:30-38). This Moabite nation became a perpetual enemy of the nation of Israel. Balak, the king of Moab, sought to curse the Israelites who were camped outside of Moab during their wilderness journey (Num 22-25). What he could not achieve with sorcery, he accomplished with seduction; a seduction that led to the deaths of 24,000 Israelites under God's judgment (Num 25:1-9). Judges 3 tells us that Moab oppressed Israel for 18 years until God delivered them through Ehud. The events told in Ruth's story take place at this point in Israel's history. Eventually, Israel's first king, Saul, defeated the Moabites and several other enemy nations in his conquests (1 Sam 14:47). Because of Saul's conquest, King David experienced peace with the Moabites; he even felt free to ask their king to protect his father and mother while he was running from Saul (1 Sam 22:1-4). Years later, Moab rebelled and unsuccessfully fought against Israel again (2 Kg 3).

The Moabites worshiped Chemosh, and God cursed them for it. Worshiping this pagan god required them to sacrifice their own children and offer them as burnt offerings. The prophets Isaiah, Jeremiah, Ezekiel, and Amos all pronounced specific judgments on the nation of Moab. This is the country to which Elimelech chose to take his family for refuge during a famine. This is the biblical account of Ruth's nation and people.

A close look at her ancestry and historical heritage illustrates the beauty of God's grace to her in colorful detail. She was a young woman from a nation of pagan customs and barbaric worship. They were known enemies of the God of Israel. Yet, Ruth is found in the ancestry of King David and the King of Kings, the Messiah. Isn't it amazing that God chooses the most unlikely people to accomplish his purposes in this world? As we "sit" with Ruth in the days ahead, let's revel in the wonderment that we ourselves experience that same grace. We, too, are the recipients of God's redemption through his Son, Jesus Christ. God is providentially working in our lives, just like he did in Ruth's. As we "listen" to Ruth, may we realize and appreciate all of the ways that her story points us to Jesus. Ruth's story is our story.

Day 2

Faith in Action

Read the entire Book of Ruth to get an overview—it will take you 10-15 minutes. As you read, place a mark in your Bible at every place in the story where you recognize God at work.

Food for Thought

- With what character or characters will you be able to most identify? Why? (gender, age, status, station in life, etc.)
- Take a few minutes to meditate on Ruth's background and the unlikeliness of her being a biblical heroine. What other biblical characters stand out in your mind as unlikely heroes used by God?

Prayer

Dear Heavenly Father, I acknowledge right now that you are the sovereign God of the universe. Your providential work is displayed throughout the pages of Scripture and throughout my world today. Give me spiritual eyes to see how you are working in my life and through my circumstances. Thank you that you never see us as unworthy recipients of your grace, no matter where we come from or what we've done. As I take a closer look at the story of Ruth, enable me to know you better and to recognize your sovereign ways in Ruth's life and my own life.

Ruth 1:1–5 and 20–22

Regret. Poor choices. Painful consequences. Loss. Loneliness. Hopelessness. Can anything good possibly come from these realities? Yes! In the merciful providence of God, he makes something beautiful out of our mistakes and our pain. Isaiah tells us that God can provide "a beautiful headdress instead of ashes, the oil of gladness instead of mourning, the garment of praise instead of a faint spirit." This is who he is and what he does. Why? "That [we] may be called oaks of righteousness, the planting of the LORD, that he may be glorified (Is 61:3)." In the following days, we will witness how Ruth's beautiful story rises from the ashes of Naomi's sorrowful one. But, we should hear Naomi's story first.

Naomi loved her husband, Elimelech. He was a God-fearer; a loving husband and father. Naomi's life was "full (1:21)" with the love of her husband and her two sons, Mahlon and Chilion. They were Israelites, God's chosen people, and Bethlehem was their home. It was the home of their extended family and friends as well. Their community and livelihood revolved around that small village.

Moral decay and political chaos were the order of the day during this time in Israel's history. Israel was in a recurring cycle of forsaking God, worshiping the false gods of the surrounding nations, experiencing the judgment of God, and then crying out to God for deliverance and mer-

> *Sometimes we rush ahead of God and try to fix our problems with a convenient, expedient solution.*

cy. Time and again. God used different calamities to discipline his people for turning their backs on him. Then, when they repented, God would raise up a judge to deliver them. War and oppression from surrounding nations led to economic crises and life-threatening existence. Tribal unrest and disunity led to devastating civil war. These were a few of the methods God used to regain the attention of his people. At the time of Elimelech and Naomi, a severe famine was causing great difficulty for the families of Bethlehem. We can assume that this famine was a result of God's judgment within this recurring cycle.

The Bible doesn't provide much backstory on Elimelech's decision to move his family from Bethlehem to Moab. So, we're left to read between the lines and speculate. Any family provider can identify with the dilemma Elimelech faced in caring for his wife and sons during this time of need. Perhaps their crops had failed and they were hungry, wondering how, when, or if the famine would end. Since friends and extended family members around them were facing the same problems, they couldn't ask anyone for help.

Perhaps Elimelech decided to find a "quick fix," the way we often do when we're confronted with a crisis. There is no indication from Scripture that he cried out to God for help or direction—he simply acted. While we're not told that his actions were made in direct disobedience to God, we can deduce that at the very least, it was not a wise decision. In the Law of Moses, the Jews were given explicit directives and warnings against interacting with pagan nations and intermarrying with those who worshiped false gods. Moab definitely fell into this category of nations. But Elimelech ignored these cautions and made the move to Moab anyway.

The Scripture states that they "went to sojourn in the country of Moab," which indicates that they intended

Day 3

the move to be temporary. Perhaps Elimelech rationalized that a temporary stay wouldn't do much harm to his family. Their temporary stay lasted at least 10 years, however. Mahlon and Chilion were young and impressionable men when they made the move. Evidently, that was not cause for concern for Elimelech. Sadly, both sons did the very thing that the law forbade; they married foreign, idol-worshiping women.

Naomi's part in the decision to leave Bethlehem is left to the imagination. But if she disagreed, it didn't change Elimelech's mind. So, she went along. As long as she was with her beloved family, she could be happy. The beginning of her sorrows began shortly after the move. Elimelech died, leaving her a widow. Despite this sadness, Naomi still had responsibilities within her family. But tragedy struck again, and death claimed both of her sons as well.

Only those who have experienced these types of devastating losses can fully empathize with her. But stop for a minute and consider how she must have felt. Away from home, family, friends. Destitute in a foreign, Godless land. The people she loved most in the world—gone from her life. What choices were left for her? What else could she do but go home? Go back with nothing. Return to face the pity of family and friends. Absorb the potential judgment and criticism of those who endured the famine in Bethlehem. Swallow the "I told you so's." Accept the consequences of her husband's poor decision. So, that is what she did—she went home.

We get a glimpse into Naomi's feelings in verses 20 and 21. She had gone away "full" and had returned "empty." She asked her friends that they no longer call her Naomi ("pleasant") but rather Mara ("bitter"). Her words in these verses testify that she believed that they had made a wrong choice. In the aftermath of that choice, she acknowledged the

> *It's easy to focus on our troubles or losses. But when we do, we fail to see the goodness of God in the midst of our difficulties.*

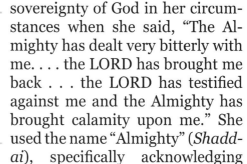

> *In the middle of our pain or regret, let's anticipate the beauty that God will bring from the ashes.*

sovereignty of God in her circumstances when she said, "The Almighty has dealt very bitterly with me. . . . the LORD has brought me back . . . the LORD has testified against me and the Almighty has brought calamity upon me." She used the name "Almighty" (*Shaddai*), specifically acknowledging that her circumstances were the result of the plan of God, not the work of chance or pagan gods. She didn't mean this as an accusation but as an acknowledgement of God's total control of all things (EBC, 525). In acknowledging the providence of God, she accepted the bitter consequences of the poor choice. We also sense the hopelessness in her voice as she anticipated in her mind a dismal future with no husband, no children, and no means.

Sometimes we rush ahead of God and try to fix our problems with a convenient, expedient solution, like Elimelech did. We fail to take time to pray, pursue God's wisdom, seek godly counsel, or consider all the ramifications of our choices. Often, we do something that seems like a great idea. Our intentions are honorable, but we haven't paused to consider if it's God's will. However well-intentioned, Elimelech went against the prescribed plan of God, and he suffered the dire consequences of moving his family to a pagan land. Ironically, the move to sustain his family's life and ensure their survival did the opposite. In the end, Naomi found herself in a strange land—a poor, childless widow.

Like Naomi, it's easy to focus on our troubles or losses. But when we do, we fail to see the goodness of God in the midst of our difficulties. While Naomi acknowledged and accepted that the negative consequences in her life were from God, she missed, at first, the beautiful blessing from God that she'd been given—her daughter-in-law, Ruth.

In the middle of our pain or regret, let's anticipate the beauty that God will bring from the ashes. Even if we've

Day 3

made a poor choice, we can trust God that he is at work. He will accomplish his purposes even through painful consequences or difficult circumstances. That's what he does!

Food for Thought

With whom do you identify in this story? Elimelech or Naomi? If you're a child of God, never forget that Christ has already paid the eternal price for your sin debt on the cross. You are forever secure from the eternal consequences of your sin and assured a place in God's family, both in this life and the life to come. Although your relationship with God is secure, your fellowship with him can be hindered by the sins and mistakes you make daily. Sometimes painful consequences follow. If you wallow in regret from the consequences of your mistakes, not only will they be painful, but also, they will be wasted, and you will be doomed to repeat them. When you wallow, you will not be able to experience the power and hope of forgiveness that Christ offers through confession. Instead of bogging down in regret, practice confession and seek God's help to learn and grow, even if painful consequences touch your life.

Remember some choices you made that brought unwanted consequences. Or, maybe, like Naomi, you have experienced pain as a result of someone else's sinful choice. Either way, did you learn anything through that difficulty about yourself or God? Acknowledge the ways that God made something beautiful from your mess.

Faith in Action

Is there a problem in your life that you're trying to fix without God? Do you tend to rush ahead to find solutions without seeking God for direction? Identify a circumstance where you might plan or act without including God in the planning or thought process.

Read the following verses: Isaiah 55:8-9; Proverbs 16:9; 19:21; 20:24; and James 4:13-16. Using these verses, write down some ways you could personally improve your perspective on choices and plans, the way you process poor choices, painful situations, difficult circumstances, and important decisions.

Day 3

Prayer

Father, too often I make bad choices when I try to do things on my own, without you. Forgive me and help me to acknowledge that your thoughts and ways are higher, wiser, and more holy than mine. I want to know you more and look to you for daily guidance. Help me to trust you in all things and to see your goodness even in difficult circumstances. Give me the desire to value your will above my own. You are God and I am not! Thank you for the promise that you can bring beauty from ashes and joy from mourning.

Day 4

Ruth 1:6–15

What comes to mind when you hear the description, "mother-in-law"? Often, society portrays these women with mostly negative stereotypes. Perhaps there's a legitimate reason why. Most married people I know have a classic, mother-in-law "story." Honestly, mothers-in-law get a bad rap, but maybe it's because some tend to be overprotective of their little boys and try to remain the most important women in their lives. Others tend to think that no man could possibly be good enough for their perfect little angels, and they spend too much time trying to convince their daughters that they deserve better. With these agendas come disapproval, snide comments, tense family gatherings, strained relationships, or worse. Displays can range from a condescending shake of the head to all out "monster-in-law" mode. While this seems to be common, Naomi and her daughters-in-law portray an exquisitely beautiful exception.

Naomi's sons married Orpah and Ruth. As a God-fearing Israelite, Naomi would not have hand-picked these Moabite girls to marry her sons. But she didn't get to choose. Her new reality was to share her family with two women from a pagan culture; women who worshiped the detestable, pagan god, Chemosh.

The normal, human response for Naomi would have been to shun Orpah and Ruth, sulking around the house while lamenting the unwise choice of her sons. She could have taken her anger and frustration out on the girls—the

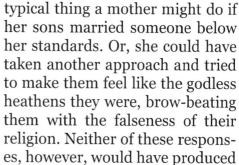

> *The life that Naomi lived in front of her daughters-in-law was one of faith, grace, and loving mentoring.*

typical thing a mother might do if her sons married someone below her standards. Or, she could have taken another approach and tried to make them feel like the godless heathens they were, brow-beating them with the falseness of their religion. Neither of these responses, however, would have produced the beautiful relationship that's described in this book.

We can be sure that the life that Naomi lived in front of her daughters-in-law was one of faith, grace, and loving mentoring. Everyone who reads this story can learn from Naomi's example and shining testimony. She lived out the reality of her faith in the presence of the pagan women who had been placed in her sphere of influence. They may not have been her choice as family members, but Naomi chose to make the most of her influence.

Imagine the feelings Orpah and Ruth must've experienced when they moved into a household where everything was different from what they knew. I'm sure they loved their husbands, but they didn't just move in with Mahlon and Chilion. They moved in with their mother-in-law—sharing space, sharing household duties, sharing everyday life. Ultimately, they all shared something that bonded them together in a unique way. They shared the grief and heartache of losing their beloved husbands. They shared the fear of what might become of them with no men and no means. And, they shared an uncertain future.

The scene in our verses today illustrates the scope of Naomi's character and the relationship she shared with her daughters-in-law. Word reached Naomi that "the LORD had visited his people and given them food (1:6)." As a result, she decided to return to her homeland. The fact that both Orpah and Ruth wanted to go with her, and were in the process of accompanying her, proves that they had a good relationship. They both initially pleaded with her to remain. They both wept at the prospect of leaving her behind. She loved them equally and sincerely. It would

Day 4

seem that her genuine love and compassionate treatment toward them made her a person for whom they were willing to leave their own family, friends, and comforts. Obviously, she had not played favorites, because they both started the journey with her.

Naomi's heart must have warmed with the thought that both of her sons' wives accompanied her willingly. I'm sure she found comfort in their desire to be with her. But as their journey began, Naomi's selflessness would not let her continue. She could have kept going, rationalizing that this was their duty. After all, if they didn't go, she would be completely alone on this arduous journey. It was within her cultural rights to have them with her. But, she loved them both and wanted what was best for them—not for herself.

Naomi's unselfish love for Orpah and Ruth shines through in the dialogue. "Go, return . . . May the LORD deal kindly with you, as you have dealt with the dead and with me. The LORD grant that you may find rest, each of you in the house of her husband (1:8-9)." She understood that they were young enough to want to marry again. "Rest" meant security, provision, blessing, and potential children. She wanted all of that for them.

Naomi's authentic faith, and her absolute trust in the providence of God, stood out against the bleak backdrop of her sad circumstances. She spoke so comfortably about her God. She asked that the LORD deal "kindly" with these two women that she loved. The Hebrew word for kindly is *chesed*. It is a complex word with rich, deep meaning. In fact, no single English word adequately describes this word. English words used to translate *chesed* are loving-kindness, mercy, and steadfast love, just to name a few. This word is used throughout the Old Testament to describe God's covenant love for his people. In Exodus 34:6-7, God used this word to describe himself

Naomi's faith, and trust in God, stood out against the bleak backdrop of her sad circumstances.

21

> Naomi understood chesed, because she understood her God.

to Moses. Psalm 136 recounts a history of how God related to his people with this "steadfast love." A simple definition would be *a faithful, loyal love demonstrated by grace and mercy and acted out by one party for the benefit of the other*. Orpah and Ruth had shown that kind of love both to Naomi and to her dead husband and sons. She desired for God to show that same loyal love to them. Naomi understood *chesed*, because she understood her God. No wonder Ruth was drawn to Naomi's faith and even embraced it as her own!

When Naomi graciously released them from their duties, they refused with tears, insisting to go with her. Verses 11-13 record Naomi's attempt to reason with the girls. She used the term of endearment "my daughters" three times as she presented both rational reasons and hypothetical scenarios about their futures. She didn't want them to share the bitter, lonely life that seemed to be facing her.

Initially, Naomi referred to the consequences of the poor choice to move to Moab in verse 13. She used the name *Yahweh*, the personal covenant name for God, to sum up her situation: "It is exceedingly bitter to me for your sake that the hand of the LORD has gone out against me." She reiterated her perspective in verse 21. While she acknowledged that God is sovereign, her focus was on the hopelessness of her situation. Naomi's declaration of hopelessness reminds us that even strong faith can have moments of weakness.

> Even strong faith can have moments of weakness.

Tears flowed again after Naomi's argument, but in the end, Orpah returned home "to her people and to her god (1:15)." Inexplicably, Ruth "clung" to Naomi. Orpah exited from the pages of

Scripture with her retreat. She is not a villain, nor did she betray Naomi in any way. However, her absence of faith stands in marked contrast to the bold, personal faith that Ruth declared and acted upon. In the end, Orpah abandoned the call to faith, because she was not willing to alter her life to act upon it.

> **Food for Thought**
>
> Look back at the paragraph that talks about the Hebrew word chesed. Read the passages given (Ex 34:6-7; Ps 136). Also read Ephesians 2:1-10 and meditate on the ways that God demonstrates chesed (loyal love or relentless love) to you.

While the narrative proves that Orpah loved Naomi, in the end, she went back to her people and to her god. This is an example of shallow faith based on the wrong things—a faith that was not her own, and as a result, could not stand the test of adversity. Maybe she just loved some people who believed in God. Maybe she was caught up in the emotions of believing, but those emotions were not enough to affect the course of her life. It appears that she was living in the reality of Naomi's faith but never embraced it for herself. Ask yourself these questions: Why do I believe? Is my faith based on emotions or someone else's faith? Do I have a personal relationship with Jesus or am I in a temporary "relationship" with religion, spirituality, or ambiguous "faith"? How do I demonstrate that my faith is real? If you cannot say that you have a personal relationship with Jesus, please read Finding L.I.F.E in Jesus at the end of this book.

Think of the people in your sphere of influence—those you chose and those you didn't. How would they characterize your faith?

Day 4

Faith in Action

Naomi's character and life of faith with her pagan daughters-in-law challenges us to be a light in our dark world—especially in our spheres of influence. Your life does make a difference! Read Matthew 5:14-16 and John 13:34-35. Write down the benefits of being a light and showing love in our world. Write down some specific ways you will shine your light and show God's love to those in your sphere of influence today.

Prayer

Father in heaven, thank you for the faithful, loyal love that you demonstrate to me every day! Even when I fail to be a light to the world, or fail to show your love to others, you love me with a love that is full of mercy and patience—a relentless love. May I not take that love for granted today. Help me to be sensitive to opportunities throughout the day, and let my light shine so that others will give you glory. Show me how I can let others know that I am your disciple by loving them.

Day 5

Ruth 1:15–20

God created us to be in relationship with him and with other people. We need God, and we need community. From the moment of our conception, our existence depends on someone else. As we grow older, we usually become more independent and can take care of ourselves. But even then, our lives are fuller and more complete when we are in relationship with other people. Even the most self-sufficient people in the world, if they're honest, would say that sharing life with other people makes life better.

Yes, relationships complicate life at times. After all, we are imperfect beings with ugly sin natures. That's why we desperately need to be in relationship with God—first and foremost. We need the supernatural in our relationships for them to have a chance at success. Even with God's help, we still struggle with sin, and it shows up most often in our relationships with other people. In spite of the complications that come from human relationships, we would still have to admit that the benefits far outweigh the challenges. The reason for this is simple: God created us to need relationships. In Ruth and Naomi, we have a beautiful example of a successful, godly relationship. Let's use the verses today to glean some perspective about what makes up a successful relationship.

It is important to note that the culture of Bible times concerning family and community is very different from our own. In Bible times, family members lived in the same house for all of their lives; they shared everything! Com-

> *God created us to be in relationship with him and with other people.*

munities of people were close-knit and dependent upon one another for the basic needs of life. Today, we are much more independent. We grow up, move out of our childhood homes, and either live by ourselves, with a family member, or with a spouse. Regardless, our goal is to be self-sufficient. Sometimes this leads us to the mistaken belief that we really don't need anyone else in our lives. But, we do!

In Day 4, we saw that Naomi had a good relationship with both of her daughters-in-law. But when circumstances dictated a major life change, their faith and relationships were tested. Orpah and Ruth had a choice to make—to stay in the comfort and familiarity of their hometown or to follow their mother-in-law to a new place, a new faith, and a new way of life. While both of them genuinely loved Naomi, and initially planned to go with her, only Ruth made the life-changing choice of faith and commitment to a life-long relationship with Naomi—and God. The words Ruth spoke in verses 16 and 17 have become an iconic example of love and commitment to God and to another person. Read her words in these verses.

As we dig a little deeper into Ruth's declaration, let's consider the deep relationships that we may have today; ones that might compare to Ruth and Naomi's. While the parallels aren't perfect, the principles of this commitment apply to any relationship, whether with a life-long friend or a close family member. It may apply best to a marriage relationship, however. This declaration of commitment contains the elements that are necessary for any deep friendship or successful marriage.

If we paraphrased Ruth's words in verses 16 and 17, it might sound something like this:

"Naomi, please don't keep trying to convince me that I am better off leaving you. I don't want to go back to my old way of life. I want to go with you. I believe God connected our lives forever when I married your son. I have

Day 5

come to love you. If I go back, I may never see you again, and I don't want that. I want to go wherever you go, even if it is difficult for me. I want to share life with you, help you, care for you, and be there for you through the good and bad of life. I will embrace your family and love them like they were my own family. I want to walk this journey of life with you until the day I die. The God you worship and serve is now my God, and I will worship and serve him until the day I die. It is because of my faith in him that I can make this commitment. In fact, I make this solemn vow that if anything but death separates me from you, may the Lord strike me dead."

Ruth's statement was so much more than a sweet cliché, easily spoken during an emotional good-bye. It was the heartfelt vow of a life-long commitment, and it included a curse if she didn't fulfill it. Her life backed up these promises with outward sacrifices of selfless action in times of difficulty and joy; a fact confirmed by the remainder of her story. Ruth's words can be boiled down to two statements of commitment:

A commitment to a shared life ... A commitment to a shared faith.

These two commitments are essential for successful relationships, especially marriage relationships. What does it mean to make a commitment to a shared life and shared faith? In a marriage, it obviously means living together—eating, sleeping, and pooling resources. But it can mean so much more. It is sharing the everyday-ness of life. Laughing together. Crying together. Working through issues, and finding solutions together. Caring for each other. Caring about each other. Listening, talking, communicating, and love-making. A shared life means that both people are headed in the same direction, with similar goals and purposes.

Ruth's statement was so much more than a sweet cliché, easily spoken during an emotional good-bye. It was the heartfelt vow of a life-long commitment.

29

> Shared faith in a marriage is foundational for success.

It is building a life together. Sharing life means accepting the things that are a part of the other person like family and important traditions. It's an understanding that says, "I want all parts of my life to include you!"

The commitment to shared faith is the most important one, however. 2 Corinthians 6:14 has this admonition, "Do not be unequally yoked with unbelievers. For what partnership has righteousness with lawlessness? Or what fellowship has light with darkness?" Since our relationship with God should be the most important thing in our life, shared faith in a marriage is foundational for success. Without it, a married couple is never really on the same page. The partners will have different priorities, goals, and perspectives on just about everything. Instead, they should share the same level of commitment to their faith. Two people who are growing in their personal relationship with God will inevitably grow closer to each other. The statement, "Your God will be my God," is the key to a successful marriage.

A commitment to a shared life and shared faith will help other relationships as well, such as life-long friendships and close family relationships. We share life with some people in the sense that they have been there for us, and will always be there for us, through the ups and downs of life. We have chosen to be in the kind of relationship that Ruth and Naomi shared. Having a shared faith with these special people in our lives is just as important. Our shared life experiences, when viewed through the lenses of a shared faith, are more meaningful and substantive.

> Two people who are growing in their personal relationship with God will inevitably grow closer to each other.

Day 5

> **Food for Thought**
>
> Think of the closest relationships in your life (i.e. spouse, best friend, business partner, close family member, etc.). Is there a spoken or unspoken commitment to a shared life and shared faith between you? Consider the benefits of that kind of commitment in that specific relationship. Think of the difficulties in a relationship where that commitment is not present.
>
> Verse 19 records a simple fact, "The two of them traveled until they came to Bethlehem." The journey from Moab to Bethlehem was at least 60-75 miles and may have taken about 7-10 days on foot. Consider how dangerous this journey must have been for two unaccompanied women. Take a moment to wonder at God's sovereign provision and protection implied here.

> **Faith in Action**
>
> Read 2 Corinthians 6:14-18 in your favorite version (reading a few other versions can be helpful too). Take a closer look at the relationships in your life that resemble Ruth and Naomi's relationship and commitment level. How do those relationships line up with the instruction in these verses and the principles implied in Ruth 1:16-17?
>
> Write or say a prayer to God, thanking him for the relationships in your life that have a commitment to a shared life and a shared faith. Then, say a prayer for the relationships in your life that should have such a commitment.

Prayer

Dear God, today I acknowledge that you created me to be in relationship with you, and that you made that relationship possible through your Son, Jesus Christ. I am so humbled and grateful that you would even desire a relationship with me, and that I receive so much grace from our relationship. I also acknowledge that you created me to need relationships with other people. Thank you for the grace you pour into my life through the people who make my life richer, as I share life and share faith with them.

Day 6

Ruth 1:22–2:4

Home sweet home! After 10 long years of being away from loved ones, friends, and the comforts of the familiar—years filled with heartache and loss—Naomi was home. It wasn't quite the homecoming she'd imagined, but she was back where she belonged. Naomi and Ruth arrived in Bethlehem at the time of year when the town was abuzz with the activities of the barley harvest. All over town, fields were ripe with barley, and the landscape was dotted with workers gleaning the crop. Landowners supervised to make sure their employees were doing their tasks. Harvesters sweated as they spent long days swinging their scythes across the fields. The backs of the gleaners ached as they continuously stooped to gather barley into their sacks. It was a meticulous process, but they had it down to a science.

In addition to paid workers, the fields were filled with the marginalized. When God gave the law to Israel, he had given specific instructions regarding the gathering of a harvest (Lev 19:9-10; 23:22; Deut 24:19-21). The law commanded that remnants of the harvest be left in the field on purpose for the poor, orphans, widows, and the sojourners to glean. Even though blessing was promised to those who obeyed, not all landowners were thrilled with this law. They would often mistreat those who would come into their fields to pick up the remnants. These laws demonstrate that God cares and provides for those in need and he wants his people to be instruments of his provision.

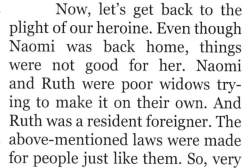

> *God provides for those in need and wants his people to be instruments of his provision.*

Now, let's get back to the plight of our heroine. Even though Naomi was back home, things were not good for her. Naomi and Ruth were poor widows trying to make it on their own. And Ruth was a resident foreigner. The above-mentioned laws were made for people just like them. So, very soon after arriving in Bethlehem, Ruth asked Naomi if she could search for a field to pick up the fallen grain that the reapers left behind for those in need. Her request showed great respect for Naomi and a humble willingness to do whatever was needed to provide for their needs. Ruth understood the custom and knew that she might not find a favorable landowner to let her glean behind the harvesters. As a Moabite foreigner, she knew her search would be even more difficult. But, with Naomi's permission, Ruth set out to take her place among those who had to depend on the kindness of others to survive.

The words in verse 3 are some of the most interesting in the book. "So she set out...and she *happened* to come to the part of the field belonging to Boaz, who was of the clan of Elimelech [emphasis mine]." This single event changed the course of Ruth and Naomi's life, even though they didn't realize it at the time. The Hebrew word *happened* literally means that "her chance chanced upon." She was a foreigner in Bethlehem and didn't know anyone except Naomi. She knew nothing of Boaz. She only knew they needed food, and she needed to find a place to get it. Out of all of the fields she could have chosen, she "chanced upon" the field that belonged to Boaz—an honorable man, a relative of her dead father-in-law, and someone who could change their lives.

What a shining example of the providence of God! What appeared to be the accidental choice of a young girl was actually the purposeful direction of God himself. God knew the plight of the helpless, God-fearing widow and the humble, young believer, and he guided Ruth's steps to

Day 6

the exact place she needed to be. Ruth was focused on the urgent, immediate need to survive. However, God led her to the field of the man who would become their kinsman redeemer. In her selfless humility, Ruth was willing to do whatever she needed to do, no matter how menial. In his divine wisdom, God guided her down a path that would lead to an exalted position as a prominent man's wife, a mother, one of the few women listed in the Messiah's genealogy, and one of two women who have a book of the Bible named for them. Amazing!

Psalms 37:23 says, "The steps of a man are established by the LORD, when he delights in his way." Proverbs 16:9 reiterates, "The heart of man plans his way, but the LORD establishes his steps." When we fear God and delight in his ways, we can rest on the promise that he will guide our steps, even our seemingly insignificant ones. We don't have to live in fear or worry about "accidents" or "bad luck." No matter what happens, we can trust that God is in the process of working all things out for our good (Rom 8:28-31). The heart that trusts that God is in control is a heart at peace, through good and bad circumstances.

Who is this man who would change the lives of Ruth and Naomi? His name is Boaz, and he enters our story in chapter 2. He is an important character in the remainder of the story. The writer of Ruth gives us a detailed description of him in 2:1. We find out right away that he was a relative of Elimelech. He is described as "a worthy man" in the ESV. A look at other versions gives us even more insight into the character of Boaz. He is described as: "a prominent man of noble character" (HCSB); "a man of great wealth" (NASB, NKJV); and "a man of standing" (NIV). The first thing we learn about Boaz is the strength of his character. He was obviously a well-respected man in the community, and he was wealthy, too. He was honorable and upright.

When we fear God and delight in his ways, we can rest on the promise that he will guide our steps, even our seemingly insignificant ones.

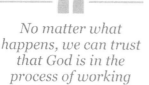

No matter what happens, we can trust that God is in the process of working all things out for our good.

While Ruth was gleaning in his field, he arrived and greeted his workers with these words, "The LORD be with you!" This phrase doesn't necessarily prove that he was a kind employer who had great respect for his employees, but their reply does. They replied with a blessing, "The LORD bless you!" In these words, we can sense harmony between the employer and employee. While it isn't always normal, this kind of harmony can be achieved when there is a mutual faith in God. A living, active faith in God should prevent the unhealthy abuse of power from a boss and disrespectful insubordination from employees.

Boaz' mutual respect and fair treatment of his employees is shown in several other places in the book as well. In Ruth 2:8-9 and 14, it is implied that he treated his harvesters and the poor gleaners with kindness and provided them with food and water. He didn't have an attitude of superiority, because he sat with his workers while they ate (2:14; 3:7). In chapter 3, we see Boaz actually working alongside his employees as they performed the physically taxing job of threshing. He led from the front—by example. Boaz was the boss everyone would love to have!

Day 6

Food for Thought

There are two ideas to ponder today. One is a theological mystery, and the other is a practical challenge.

First, think about all of the times that you use the words "by chance," "lucky," "it just so happened," "as fate would have it," and "accident." Do you really believe that things happen randomly? Are we really just victims of chance, fate, or karma? How does today's scene in the story challenge your thoughts about the way decisions and events play out in your life?

Second, if you are in the work force, what can you learn from Boaz' dealings with his employees? What is needed in the way you lead others and work with others? What can you do to improve your attitude toward your co-workers and/or your boss?

Faith in Action

Read Psalms 37:23 and Proverbs 16:9 again. Acknowledge "divine appointments" in your life today. Live with the awareness that God is at work all around you—in your life, in others' lives, in the big picture stuff, and even in the details. Be intentional about looking for God's providential hand. Write down some specific ways you can train your mind to acknowledge that God is in control.

If you are an employer, a boss, team leader, or manager, find some specific traits in Boaz that you will try to emulate. Do you need to show your employees more respect or kindness? Do you need to be more sensitive to what they need so that they can perform their jobs better? Do you need to be more willing to lead from the front instead of driving from the back? Are you a boss that others easily respect because you are a person of character and kindness? Write down some specific things that you will work to improve. Maybe *you just need to realize that within the providence of God, he has placed your co-workers around you for a divine purpose. Look for that purpose and be a part of what God is doing around you.*

One last thing. You may not be a boss at this point of your life. However, you can learn something from today's story as well. Remember, the people who worked for Boaz respected him. Regardless of whether you like your boss or not, you can honor Christ through your work. Paul wrote, "Whatever you do, work heartily, as for the Lord and not for men, knowing that from the Lord you will receive the inheritance as your reward. You are serving the Lord Christ (Col 3:23-24)."

Prayer

Father, give me eyes to see you at work around me. As I strive to walk with you each day, make me aware that every step in my life is under your control. May my actions towards my co-workers, and even the marginalized around me, reflect my belief that you care for them and are at work in their lives as well. Give me peace as I trust that you are working every circumstance in my life "for good," so that I will "be conformed to the image of [your] son (Rom 8:28-29)."

Day 7

Ruth 2:5–13

For all the chick-flick lovers out there, you know the scene (cue romantic love song). The leading man looks across the room and sees the girl. Smitten by her breath-taking beauty, he watches her longingly, asks his friends who she is, and then frantically brainstorms a way to meet her. Gathering his courage, he timidly approaches her. And when their eyes meet, something magical happens—love takes flight! Aww, we love it!

The technical term for this moment in the movies is the "meet-cute." It's that moment when the guy and girl meet for the first time. Every love story has a meet-cute. At this precise moment, those of us with romantic souls can be swept away to our fantasy world of perfect, romantic dreams; where love is as easy as that. Those with less romantic leanings may find themselves a little nauseous and overcome with skepticism. Today, we will look at Boaz and Ruth's meet-cute. This is one that will have us all cheering for love.

The scene takes place in Boaz' barley field in Bethlehem. Ruth had been gleaning behind the harvesters since early morning. She was undoubtedly exhausted. Her hair and clothes were soaked with sweat, and she probably smelled of the field. However, she remained at her task, driven

Ruth was respectful of the customs in her new land and wanted to be sure that she was going about things the correct way.

She was also a young woman who was not afraid of hard work and sweat.

by the desire to provide food for Naomi and herself.

Boaz had just arrived to see how the harvest was going. As he looked over his fields, his eyes were drawn to a young woman who looked out of place among the other gleaners. She was young, unusually beautiful to his eyes, and obviously not from Bethlehem. I would imagine it was her appearance that caught his eye. That's usually how it works with men. However, it could've been the diligent way that she was working. At any rate, Boaz was so intrigued that he had to know who she was; so he asked his foreman.

The foreman informed his boss that she was the Moabite woman that everyone was talking about—the girl who came back to town with Naomi. He reported further that she had asked permission to follow the harvesters and pick up the fallen grain. Perhaps he mentioned this fact because it was unnecessary to receive permission to do this. Everyone knew that the law gave her the right to do so. He must have been impressed that Ruth asked. He also added that she had been working constantly since early morning with only one small rest.

While this report was typical, it does reveal a few more characteristics about our heroine. Ruth was respectful of the customs in her new land and wanted to be sure that she was going about things the correct way. She was also a young woman who was not afraid of hard work and sweat. Both of these attributes caught the attention and admiration of the foreman, who then pointed them out to Boaz.

The moment had arrived. Boaz had to meet this young woman. The Scriptures don't let us in on his thoughts or motives, but we can read between the lines. We can

He said what every woman longs to hear from her man—that he saw who she was, he understood and acknowledged her, and he valued her.

Day 7

be sure that a man of Boaz' prominence did not try to meet all of the needy young women that came to his fields, but he wanted to meet this one. He had actually heard about her in the news around town, but had not yet seen her or Naomi. Since he was probably older than Ruth (3:10), we can't be sure if it was romantic attraction or familial protection that he felt most at the time, but perhaps one grew out of the other: attraction or the need to protect—both are equally endearing.

Boaz approached Ruth and immediately revealed his attraction to her and his desire to care for her in his instructions. He told her, "I would like for you to stay and work in *my* fields. Don't go to any other. Please stay close to *my* personal servant girls. Wherever they are harvesting, I want you to glean behind them. That way, you will be safe. Furthermore, I have given special instructions to the men that they are to treat you appropriately and with high regard. I know that you'll get thirsty out here in the fields. When you do, I want you to drink directly from the jars that *my* men have filled for themselves."

Unaware of Boaz' earlier interest and inquiry, Ruth bowed with humility, perplexed by the attention of the boss. She marveled at his kindness toward a foreigner such as herself. Why would he offer her privileges not offered to others? She was probably mortified by her looks and scent after hours of work in the field. And surely her heart raced at the special attention and tenderness from such a man.

Boaz told her that he had heard the good things that people said about her. He said what every woman longs to hear from her man—that he saw who she was, he understood and acknowledged her, and he valued her. She didn't know it, but her reputation and selfless care of Naomi had spread throughout the community and reached his ears. Boaz acknowledged her sacrifice in leaving the comforts of her own home to embrace the foreign customs of another. He pro-

Ruth was overwhelmed by Boaz' favor.

"You have comforted me and spoken to the heart of your slave."

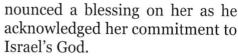

nounced a blessing on her as he acknowledged her commitment to Israel's God.

Ruth was overwhelmed by Boaz' favor. She understood that he was treating her in a special way, even though she was lower than his female servants. She expressed, "You have comforted me and spoken to the heart of your slave." Yes, Boaz definitely got off on the right foot in this budding relationship.

In the next few days, Boaz and Ruth's love story will unfold in all of its awkward and sweet entirety. But it all began when God sovereignly guided Ruth's steps to Boaz' barley field, where they would finally meet face to face—a divinely directed meet-cute.

Day 7

Food for Thought

We've walked through the scene, but can we learn anything from it today? It can be more than just a sweet story, although we should simply appreciate a sweet story, especially one orchestrated by God. But here are a few thoughts to ponder.

If you are an unmarried woman, this story may once again stir your longing for God to bring your Boaz to you. If you are begging God to reveal his will, remember that he works in the midst of the mundane. Most often, he reveals his will while you are being faithful in the daily things and striving to please him. Ruth wasn't in pursuit of a man. It was probably the last thing in her sweat-soaked head. She was busy doing what she was supposed to do, and God supernaturally guided her steps to the right place at the right time. Keep praying and keep committing your ways to the Lord. Get out there and do what God wants you to do. "If onlys" can paralyze you, make you discontent, and keep you from living the life God has for you. Finding a man should never be the ultimate goal of your life—glorifying God with your life should be. Allowing God to fulfill his purposes in your life brings the greatest joy, no matter your personal status.

If you are an unmarried man, you can learn a few things from Boaz today, too. Boaz was unafraid to approach the woman that caught his attention. When he did talk to her, he did several things that were sure to impress the sandals off of Ruth. He spoke to her with tenderness and kindness, expressing his desire to care for and protect her. He complimented her selfless actions. He noticed and acknowledged who she was and what she was doing. He valued her character and expressed it in words. He definitely passed the Chivalry 101 class! Don't be paralyzed by the fear of rejection. Step up and be the man God wants you to be, and the right woman will notice and *appreciate it. For you married guys, let me encourage you to take a page out of Boaz' playbook. Value your wife daily, and express your appreciation for her. Treat her with kindness, tenderness, and care. You won't regret it!*

Ladies, Ruth's reputation got Boaz' attention. She stood out for her selflessness and sacrifice. Her work ethic was exemplary, while her strength and humility made people take notice. She was probably the "talk of the town." However, it seems that people had nothing but good things to say about her. As a foreigner, you know that if there had been anything negative to say, it would've spread quickly and widely. She seemed to be above reproach. Proverbs 22:1 says that a good reputation is far more valuable than wealth. Proverbs 31:30 reminds us that charm and beauty can be deceptive and temporary, but the woman who fears the Lord will be praised. What can you learn from these characteristics of Ruth today?

Faith in Action

Boaz revealed his own deep faith in his pronouncement of blessing on Ruth. He described the God of Israel with the same imagery that is used in the Books of the Law. He was obviously familiar enough with these Scriptures to use them with Ruth. Read Exodus 19:3-6 and Deuteronomy 32:11. What is the image used in these verses to describe God's care and providence? Perhaps Boaz himself taught these Scriptures to his great grandson, David, who penned them in his own words in Psalm 91:4. "He will cover you with his feathers, and under his wings you will find refuge." Write down some ways that this imagery encourages you today.

Day 7

Prayer *Father in heaven, thank you for the faithful, loyal love that you demonstrate to me every day! Even when I fail to be a light to the world, or fail to show your love to others, you love me with a love that is full of mercy and patience—a relentless love. May I not take that love for granted today. Help me to be sensitive to opportunities throughout the day, and let my light shine so that others will give you glory. Show me how I can let others know that I am your disciple by loving them.*

Day 8

Ruth 2:14–23

    Boaz and Ruth's first date wasn't spectacular, but it was sweet. It wasn't filled with sparkling conversation or daring adventure; it was simply a satisfying meal with good company, chaperones included. Boaz asked Ruth to join him (and the harvesters) for lunch. He made sure she had a good dipping sauce for her bread (which is so important), and he personally served her some specially roasted grain. She even had enough to leave with a doggie bag.

    Boaz must've enjoyed his lunch with Ruth and become even more enamored with her. After she left, he made special arrangements with his harvesters to provide more grain for Ruth, while allowing her to keep her dignity as a gleaner. He asked them to let her glean right up among the bundles, not just from a distance, as was the usual method. He even ordered them to pull out some extra grain from the bundles for her to gather, and he told them not to humiliate or rebuke her for this. If Boaz had simply given the grain to her it would have been charity, and Ruth may have been offended. He understood that Ruth wanted to work hard to gather as much as she could, because she felt responsible for Naomi.

    Ruth must have wondered why the harvesters were dropping so much grain. She was so unfamiliar with the process, that she probably wasn't aware that she was doing anything unusual by gleaning so close to the bundles. She was just excited that she was gathering so much grain for

Naomi quickly acknowledged God's hand in this divine appointment.

her and Naomi. At the end of the day, she threshed her grain and it came close to 50 pounds. That's amazing, considering that the average ration of a male worker was about one to two pounds of grain per day (EBC, 532).) She was in "beast mode!"

She must've been so excited to show Naomi what she had accomplished and provided for them. She was even able to share her doggie bag from lunch with her. Naomi was amazed and realized right away that something extraordinary had happened. Someone had taken notice of her daughter-in-law and blessed her above and beyond the norm.

Innocently, and without knowing the connection herself, she told her mother-in-law about her day. It may have gone something like this: "Yes, I found this great field where the nicest people worked. They weren't very efficient though, because they kept dropping grain from the bundles, so I just picked them up. It's how I got so much. AND, I even got to meet the owner of the field. He came to talk to me and asked me to lunch. I was a filthy mess, but he showed such kindness to me. I didn't know what to make of it, but it made me feel very special. He seemed like such a wonderful man. He said that he's heard of us. Maybe you know him? His name was Boaz."

Naomi couldn't believe her ears. She blessed his heart, but genuinely—not the Southern way. She quickly acknowledged God's hand in this divine appointment and referenced God's promise never to forsake the "living or the dead." Naomi's faith in the providence of God shone through her response. She identified this man as a close relative and one who could serve as a family redeemer. Ruth may not have understood what Naomi was saying in this reply, but Naomi's heart must have skipped a beat with the sudden glimmer of hope for herself and her beloved daughter-in-law.

Day 8

Ruth joined in Naomi's excitement and added that Boaz wanted her to remain in his fields for the duration of the harvest. Naomi gave her hearty approval, and Ruth stayed in Boaz' fields until the barley and wheat harvests were over, which was usually a span of seven weeks. We are left to wonder how much interaction took place between Boaz and Ruth during that time. Surely, his obvious interest and care for her provision and protection continued. Maybe there were more lunch dates or field-side conversations.

Naomi identified Boaz as a kinsman redeemer (2:20). This is the first time this word is used in this book, but an understanding of it is vital to the story. The Hebrew word is *goel*, the root of which means to redeem, or buy back. The nearest kin had the first option to act according to the Levirate law.

According to Scripture, there were three requirements for someone to act as a kinsman redeemer: 1) The kinsman redeemer must be a blood relative (Lev 25:25); 2) He must have the necessary means and resources to act (Lev 25:35, 48-49); 3) There must be a willingness to act (Deut 25:7) (MBC, 292). He was not required by law to do anything, but he could if he so desired.

The Bible also details the various ways that a kinsman redeemer could act to help a family member: 1) The law allowed the kinsman redeemer to be a guiltless avenger of a murder committed against a family member (Num 35:12-24; Deut 19:6, 12); 2) The kinsman redeemer could also choose to be a rescuer. If he so desired, he could marry the widow of a family member to rescue her family from anonymity and to protect her from being desolate and alone. This act ensured that the family name of the deceased family member would continue. It also guaranteed that the widow would be cared for and protected in a time when widows were extremely vulnerable (Deut 25:5-10); 3) He could choose

Kinsman Redeemer: The Hebrew word is goel, the root of which means to redeem, or buy back.

> A willing and able kinsman redeemer could be a real hero and beneficiary to a family in need.

to be a restorer of lost property. If he had the means, he could opt to buy back any property that was sold by a family member to pay a debt (Lev 25:23-28); 4) He could be a redeemer of lost freedom. He could pay the ransom for a family member who had been sold into slavery to pay debts (Lev 25:47-49). A willing and able kinsman redeemer could be a real hero and beneficiary to a family in need.

In chapter 4, Boaz had the opportunity to fulfill the role of kinsman redeemer for Naomi and Ruth. We will review how this plays out in the coming days. In this way, he is a type of Christ, who fulfills the role of kinsman redeemer for us. Jesus Christ is the perfect kinsman redeemer. He meets the requirements to be one, and he acts in every way that a kinsman redeemer is allowed.

Read the Scriptures below and compare the following truths to the four ways listed above that a kinsman redeemer can act. One day in the future, Jesus will avenge us by defeating our enemy, Satan (Rom 16:20). Christ rescued and delivered us from the power of sin, death, and the grave (1 Cor 15:55-57). He redeemed us from our bondage to sin and offers us freedom like we could never experience without him (Jn 8:34-36; Gal 5:1). He moved us from darkness to light and gave us special status (1 Pet 2:8-9). He gives us everything we need for life (2 Pet 1:3-4).

Day 8

Food for Thought

Take some time to ponder these truths and "praise the One who paid [your] debt and raised [your] life up from the dead (Jesus Paid it All by Kristian Stanfill)."

Faith in Action

Review these New Testament verses and write down how these verses point to Jesus Christ's fulfillment as our kinsman redeemer.

- Must be a blood relative. Gal 4:4-5; Heb 2:11-17

- Must have the necessary means and resources. 1 Cor 6:20; 1 Pet 1:18-19

- Must have a willingness to be the kinsman redeemer. Mt 20:28; Jn 10:14-18; Titus 2:14

Prayer

Dear Jesus, I love how these stories in the Old Testament point to you and the truths of the gospel. You saw me and knew my need for a redeemer. You paid my sin debt. You rescued and delivered me from my hopelessness and my bondage to sin and self. Through your sacrifice, you restored me to a right relationship with God, gave me a new identity, and called me your own. Thank you, Jesus, for choosing to be my kinsman redeemer!

Ruth 3:1–6

So far, we have witnessed Boaz and Ruth's love awaken, through the meet-cute, the first date, the special gifts and caring, and Boaz' invitation to Ruth into his world and his community. We have reached the climax of the story — the "will-they-or-won't-they-end-up-together"— part of the story. So far, Boaz has made all of the moves towards Ruth, and every nuance of the narrative screams that he is falling for her. Yet, in his culture there was only so much that he could do. Since he was perhaps 20 years older than Ruth, it would not have been proper for him to initiate a proposal. But don't worry--Naomi had a plan. Sometimes, couples just need a little push.

From the moment Naomi learned that God put Ruth right smack in the middle of Boaz' fields, she began to put feet to her prayers. Ruth 1:9 told us Naomi's prayer and desire for her daughters-in-law, "The LORD grant that you may find rest, each of you in the house of her husband!" In Ruth 3:1 she said to Ruth, "My daughter, should I not seek *rest* for you, that it may be well with you? [emphasis mine]"

We know that Ruth needed physical rest and a serious vacation after weeks of back-breaking gleaning, but this was not the kind of rest Naomi sought for her beloved Ruth. The Hebrew word for *rest* involves security; a state of contentment and satisfaction expected to be found in marriage. This was the kind of rest she desired for her daughter-in-law. Sadly, those words don't describe the

> *From the moment Naomi learned that God put Ruth right smack in the middle of Boaz' fields, she began to put feet to her prayers.*

majority of marriages today. Think how different marriages would be if husbands and wives would strive towards this ideal, for the glory of God.

Naomi observed the budding romance between Boaz and Ruth from a distance. In her wisdom and experience, she knew that Ruth was the object of Boaz' affections. Arranged marriages were the norm, and she knew that it was time to do some arranging. I imagine her conversation with Ruth went like this: "Isn't it time for me to make sure that you find the security, contentment, and care that I've prayed about for you? How about Boaz? He's our relative. He obviously cares about you. Look at all he has done for you and for us. He made sure that you kept working in his fields with his personal servants, for goodness sakes. I have a plan and I need for you to trust me."

John Piper calls Naomi's plan "strategic righteousness." This is in contrast to the "passive righteousness" demonstrated by not murdering, not stealing, and not doing something wrong (Crossway; July 15, 1984; Used by permission, 2012). Strategic righteousness is taking right action. Naomi prayed for Ruth to find rest in the home of a husband, and then she played a role in making it happen. This is a beautiful picture of divine sovereignty and human responsibility working together to accomplish God's purposes. God created the opportunity, and Naomi acted on it.

Naomi gave Ruth very specific instructions about what she was supposed to do. Her instructions can be paraphrased into something that may have sounded like this: "Ruth honey, the first thing you need to do is take a good long bath. Wash all that grime and

> *The Hebrew word for rest involves security; a state of contentment and satisfaction expected to be found in marriage.*

Day 9

sweat off and don't forget to get the dirt out from under your fingernails. After your bath, put on some of that lavender oil so that you smell pretty. Wear that dress that brings out the color in your eyes and take the matching jacket—you're going to need it tonight. I may be old, but I still know a thing or two about men. Of course, you are beautiful all the time, even when you're sweaty, but it doesn't hurt to let a man know that you've made an effort to look your best."

She continued, "Boaz is finishing up the harvest at the threshing floor tonight, so I want you to go down there. Find some place where you won't be seen by Boaz or his workers. Hang out there until they have finished working, eating, and drinking. Trust me, it's never good to have a serious talk with a man while he's working, eating, or watching sports. They will all sleep at the threshing floor, so wait until they've all gone to bed."

Then came the interesting part, "What I'm asking you to do next sounds crazy, I know, but I need you to trust me. Make sure you notice exactly where Boaz lies down and let him go to sleep. If you go to the wrong man, it's going to be downright awkward, so make sure you know! When you find Boaz, go to his bed, gently uncover his feet—only his feet I tell you—and lie down at the end of his bed. Then wait, and he will tell you what to do next. I know, I know, it all sounds so strange, but trust me, and follow my instructions explicitly."

At this point, Ruth could have protested profusely and made a note to call the local mental-health facility about Naomi. We wouldn't have blamed her. Goodness, we would've helped her find the number. This plan sounds absolutely ludicrous to us, and it probably did to Ruth, too. However, the process of uncovering someone's feet was a custom indicating a marriage proposal in the ancient Near East. It doesn't sound nearly as romantic as a man getting down

> *Think how different marriages would be if husbands and wives would strive towards this ideal, for the glory of God.*

This is a beautiful picture of divine sovereignty and human responsibility working together to accomplish God's purposes.

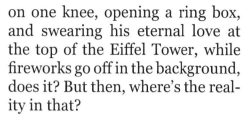

on one knee, opening a ring box, and swearing his eternal love at the top of the Eiffel Tower, while fireworks go off in the background, does it? But then, where's the reality in that?

Ruth's response was indicative of her character. She loved Naomi. She trusted her. She was submissive and humble. And most importantly, she was teachable and willing to follow wise counsel. She replied, "All that you say I will do. So she went down to the threshing floor and did just as her mother-in-law had commanded her (3:5-6)."

Well, the first step had been taken—this was the point of no return. Ruth had to really put herself out there. Boaz would have to respond. If we didn't know the end of the story already, we might be really nervous, even embarrassed, for Ruth at this point. But we will pretend that this is the cliffhanger, and we will have to tune in tomorrow to find out what happened. "As sands in the hourglass of time . . . so goes the Days of Our Lives."

Day 9

Food for Thought

What are some lessons that we can learn from Ruth's attitude and actions in our reading today? She listened to Naomi's wise counsel, trusting her spiritual maturity and love. She didn't argue or present a better plan. She was teachable. Are you? How well do you listen? Do you always have a plan and push your plan? Do you have a spiritually mature person in your life that you allow to give you counsel?

Look closely at Naomi's actions. She acknowledged God's sovereign guidance and provision in their lives, but didn't just sit back passively. God used her as the catalyst in this budding romance. She was a willing participant in God's sovereign work, and she received blessings and benefits from being God's vessel. Are you willing to join God in what he is doing in the lives of those around you? Do you pray that God will reveal opportunities for you to participate in what he is doing?

How about Boaz? These verses portray another great example of modeling servant leadership. Once again, we see him working alongside his men, not just pushing them from the sidelines. He wasn't pretentious or too proud to associate with his workers. Does this example speak to you in any area of your life—in your marriage, at your job, or in your church?

Faith in Action

1) Rate yourself on how teachable you are or how well you listen to counsel. Which of the following best describes you?
- I need no improvement. I got this. I don't let anyone tell me anything. I can't remember the last time I listened to someone else and followed their advice (You need much improvement!

> Humble yourself before God, and ask him to forgive you. Acknowledge your need for God's help, and ask him to transform your heart and make it teachable. He is waiting for you to turn to him for help!).

- *I need to be more intentional about improvement. It's not that I'm not willing to follow counsel, but I don't find myself seeking godly counsel. I try to figure things out on my own.* (At least you admit that you need to take steps to improve. That's a positive sign! God wants to make you into a willing vessel. Ask him to show you how you can be more teachable.)
- *I can always stand to improve in this area. I realize my need for accountability and seek wise counsel from spiritually mature people on a regular basis. I understand fully that I don't know everything and have much room to grow and learn.* (You've got it! You are a teachable person. You are a vessel that God can and will use. Ask him to continue to work in your life—teaching you and growing you into a person he can use.)

2) Ask yourself this question: Do you think that God is totally responsible for all that happens? Or do you think that man is held responsible for his actions and the choices in his life? If your answer is "Yes" to both questions, then you acknowledge the parallel truths of God's sovereignty and man's responsibility in this world. While it may seem impossible for both to be correct, the Scriptures clearly teach that both are equally true. Instead of fighting it or arguing about it, live in simple trust that God is in control, and strive to follow God's word and make life choices that will bring him glory.

Prayer

Thank you, Father, for the example of Ruth, who was humbly teachable; for Naomi, who was "strategically righteous" in joining you in your sovereign work; and for Boaz, who exemplified servant leadership. Help me to acknowledge my need to grow and learn. Make me teachable and willing to follow godly counsel. I acknowledge your complete sovereignty over all the affairs of my life, but desire to be a willing participant of what you are doing in my life and the lives of those in my sphere of influence—for your glory!

Day 10

Ruth 3: 7–18

Welcome back! What happens next in our story will determine not only the future of the nation of Israel and every believer who will ever live, but also whether God will fulfill his covenant promises. Kind of a big deal, right? It's decision time—"put-up or shut-up"—time for action. We have already established that God is entirely sovereign, but we have also determined that man is responsible for his actions, and God uses those actions to accomplish his sovereign work. As mind blowing as that is, we see it playing out right here in these verses.

Naomi crafted a plan based on her assessment of what had taken place between Ruth and Boaz and what God had already done. In verse 6, Ruth was waiting on Boaz to fall asleep so that she could carry out Naomi's plan. We can only imagine what was going through her mind and how nervous she must have been. It was plain to see that Boaz cared for her, but would such a great and influential man want to marry a Moabitess? Her beloved Naomi had put all her hopes in this plan for a better future for them. She hadn't seen Naomi this happy and hopeful since Moab—before all the loss. All they could do was trust that God was up to something; they were just joining him. Her trust in God and Naomi gave feet to her faith.

In "stealth mode," Ruth approached Boaz after he had fallen asleep, "uncovered his feet and lay down (3:7)." What a bold and suggestive move! Like most men who have worked hard all day and have a full belly, Boaz was

> *God is entirely sovereign, but we have also determined that man is responsible for his actions, and God uses those actions to accomplish his sovereign work.*

out—dead asleep. He probably would've slept all night if something hadn't startled him around midnight. Maybe it was God who gave him that little nudge to get the ball rolling. When he sat up, he saw her—so young and beautiful. He had fallen for her, but he never thought he'd have a chance with her. He had taken care of her, provided for her, and protected her, but he had only dreamed that she would let him love her.

Ruth wasted no time with coyness or confusing flirtation. She identified herself and came right to the point. She respected his previous loving intentions and was forthright with her own. She made this request, "Spread your wings over your servant, for you are a redeemer (3:9)."

Remember Ruth 2:12, where Boaz asked the LORD to bless and reward Ruth, because she was seeking refuge under his wings? In 3:9, Ruth essentially said, "Boaz, *you* may be the answer to your own prayer for me. *You* can be the agent of God's reward to me. Yes, I seek refuge under God's wings, and *you* can be God's 'wings of refuge' for me."

We can almost hear the wheels in Boaz' head turning as his heart pounded. This beautiful young woman, who had caught his attention and captured his heart, had just asked him to marry her—to be her redeemer. This woman, who was so selfless in her kindness to her mother-in-law, and who was humbly unaware that she could get any younger man she wanted, had come to him. He answered with a resounding, "Yes, I will do it all!" Isn't it endearing that he recognized and acknowledged her feelings and her fears? Then, he valued her when he told her that all "know that you are a worthy woman (3:11)."

> *"Spread your wings over your servant, for you are a redeemer."*

Day 10

Verses 12-13 demonstrate Boaz's integrity. Even though he was dying for the chance to be the one to redeem Ruth and Naomi, he knew that he was not the first in line for that responsibility. Still, he assured her that he would take care of things from that point on and do all that he could do to make sure they were provided for. Selfishly, he could have taken what he wanted to satisfy his desires, but the well-being of Ruth and Naomi triumphed over that desire. What a beautiful picture of unselfish love!

While his integrity dictated that he had to work through the Levitical process, his passion shone through when he made the most solemn and binding oath a Hebrew could make. Notice verse 13, "But if he is not willing to redeem you, then, *as the LORD lives*, I will redeem you [emphasis mine]." To invoke God's name and not fulfill the oath would have been a violation of the third commandment (EBC, 538). Boaz told Ruth how he felt and what his intentions were.

Boaz requested that Ruth stay the rest of the night. I want more details here, don't you? Did they get any sleep the rest of the night? Probably not. Did they reminisce about how God had led their paths together? Maybe. Did their hearts race with desire and anticipation? Most likely. Did they lose self-control under the canopy of stars that night? Absolutely not! These romantic circumstances could have naturally led to a sexual encounter if Boaz had not been a noble man and Ruth a virtuous woman. For some interpreters to suggest such a thing is ludicrous to me, and it appears to be completely contradictory to the character traits of Boaz and Ruth that are portrayed in the book. Even though the Bible condemns sex outside of marriage, the Scriptures don't hesitate to describe sexual encounters when they occurred—good or bad. This is clearly a description of the opposite. Boaz took care that their good standing and reputation were preserved.

> *God makes his people holy and then says, "Now, go live like it. Be the person I made you to be."*

63

> *Naomi, the one with the voice of wisdom and experience, recognized that they had done all they could do. The rest was in God's hands.*

Boaz sent Ruth back home with a shawl full of barley for Naomi. This act of kindness was ripe with meaning. He provided a gift for Naomi as an acknowledgment of her significance in the process. It may have also served as a kind of down-payment for the promise he made. He wanted her to know that they had a willing, kinsman redeemer. At the very least, it was another demonstration of his desire to care and provide for Ruth and Naomi.

Meanwhile, Naomi was probably watching for Ruth by the window. She probably spent the night going over possible scenarios and outcomes, interspersed with hope-filled prayers. After all, their futures would be determined by what happened. When she saw Ruth, she probably ran to meet her and said, "I want to know ALL the details." Ruth obliged and "told her all (3:16)." This scene is a testament to the close relationship that they had, and it can best be understood by two friends who love one another and want to know every detail of each other's lives.

Naomi told Ruth to "wait (3:18)." Naomi, the one with the voice of wisdom and experience, recognized that they had done all they could do. The rest was in God's hands. This instruction from Naomi proved that she had learned to trust God with outcomes, results, and answers. She did not formulate another plan to go behind Boaz and make sure he was doing his part. She didn't display an attitude of worry over what would happen to them. She didn't call her friends to find out how things were progressing. She said, "Let's wait, be patient, and relax. God has this! I have a confident expectation that Boaz will keep his promise. Just you wait and see."

Day 10

Food for Thought In this world of sexual promiscuity, Boaz and Ruth shine as an example of righteousness, purity, and self-control. Too many think that sex is a foregone conclusion in any relationship—something that just naturally happens and can't be helped. To think otherwise, they say, is archaic and unrealistic. Some even go so far as to rationalize that God created us with sexual urges, so he must understand how impossible it is to ignore them. In other words, they think God's commands for sexual purity are culturally irrelevant. Have you ever entertained these thoughts? Do you know someone who struggles with these ideas?

Faith in Action God is holy and pure, and he demands holiness and purity from his children. While his grace and mercy are offered freely to us because of our depraved, sinful natures, his desire for our purity doesn't change, because he cannot change. Our sinful nature neither negates nor nullifies his holy nature. "To equate any and every personal sexual desire as natural, healthy, and God-given is a powerful lie (The Woman's Study Bible. "Sexual Purity: Passion Held By Principle." Nashville: Thomas Nelson Publishers, 1995. 1904)." While it is true that God created you with natural, sexual desires, you must only exercise them according to his will within the marriage relationship; to do otherwise is to sin. If you've been struggling with sexual sin, now is the time to confess that sin and run from it. Look up the following verses and commit anew to purity in your heart and life: 1 Thessalonians 4:3-8 and Titus 2:12-14.

Now, look at the example of Naomi's confident faith at the end of this chapter. She possessed a faith that was able to wait for God to accomplish his purposes. She had done her part and encouraged Ruth to do hers—join God in what he was already doing. Then, she ceased her striving to allow God to do what only he could do. Her hope was in God (Rom 15:13).

Are there any areas of your life where you need to stop trying to work things out the way you think they should happen? Is God trying to tell you to "wait (Is 40:31)?" Is he saying, "Stand still and see this great thing that the LORD will do before your eyes (1 Sam 12:16; cf Ex 14:13; 2 Chr 20:17)."

These two concepts are interconnected as well. Are you sinfully pursuing sexual happiness at the cost of your personal purity? Why not look to the one who can give you lasting joy, not just momentary satisfaction? Obey God, wait, and watch him fulfill his purposes in your life.

Prayer

Our Father in heaven, holy is your name! Don't let me forget that. Forgive my wandering heart. Forgive my sinful rationalizations. Help me to keep my eyes fixed on you, so that I won't focus on the wrong things. Keep my thoughts and actions pure. You are at work in my life and in my heart, and I trust that. Forgive me when I choose my own way and pursue my own desires. I submit to you. I want to obey you and then wait to see you do what only you can do.

Day 11

Ruth 4:1–12

The world we live in today looks very different from the world of Ruth and Naomi. It's hard for us to fully understand how dire their circumstances truly were. In the world in which we live, women have powerful positions in business and government. We watch women who are widows, single mothers, married, or unmarried, live independent, successful lives. In our western world, women can vote, own property or businesses, inherit family fortunes, and enjoy equality with men on nearly every level. Our culture even preaches "Girl power" and "Girls Rule!" While there is still a glass ceiling, as women, "We've come a long way, baby."

Ruth and Naomi were women who lived in a man's world, however. Women had no legal rights. They survived at the mercy of others—husbands, family members, or generous friends. Women had no legal possessions. Apparently, Elimelech had sold the family land to be able to move to Moab. Naomi had no ability or right to redeem it back on her own. Women in that day held no position. Naomi had no standing in the community that afforded her assistance or provision. In a land where having a husband and children gave you significance, she had neither. In a culture where your inheritance and future were dependent on offspring, she was old and past her child-bearing years. Naomi and Ruth were alone, and they only had each other. They faced anonymity, poverty, and extinction, trapped in their unfortunate circumstances. They desperately need-

> *Naomi and Ruth were alone, they desperately needed a savior, a redeemer, a rescuer.*

ed a savior, a redeemer, a rescuer. Their lives and their futures depended on the outcome of Boaz's quest.

Thankfully, Naomi was right. Boaz let no grass grow under his feet. He went to Bethlehem's city gate at his first opportunity and waited for the man with whom he needed to discuss his business. It was the custom of the day to make business transactions and settle disputes at the city gate. It functioned as the city hall, city court, and chamber of commerce all rolled into one. We can sense Boaz's eagerness to make this transaction, one way or the other. The unnamed, nearest-of-kin came through the gate, and Boaz pulled him aside. Next, Boaz called together ten elders to oversee and witness the matter—this was a big deal! Finally, it was time for Boaz to make the proposition. It may have gone something like this:

"I need you to make a decision that concerns one of our family members. You know Naomi, who has recently returned from Moab. Her late husband Elimelech sold their land before they moved. She's back with no husband and no children and needs a kinsman redeemer to buy it back for the sake of the family's name and inheritance. You're the first in line. Would you be willing? We have the witnesses we need here. If you are willing, redeem it today. If not, then I'm next in line and will do it myself."

"Sure, I'll redeem it," the nearest of kin replied nonchalantly. Perhaps he thought to himself, "Who wouldn't want more land? It can be Naomi's inheritance for a while. But she's old, and it'll pass to me and my children soon enough."

Boaz quickly added, "Alright, but you should know that part of the deal is that you must marry Ruth, the Moabite widow of Mahlon, so that you can carry on the name of his family and increase their inheritance. After

Day 11

all, that's the requirement of a kinsman redeemer, as you know."

There must have been a pause while the man considered the new consequences of this choice. Then he replied, "Uh . . . I can't do it then. I'm not willing to split my own children's inheritance with children who carry another man's name. You can have my right of redemption for yourself."

As strange as it may seem, the deal was sealed with the passing of a shoe (4: 7-8). This symbolized the act by one person of giving up the right of possession to another, and the right of the new owner to set foot on the land (*Unger's Bible Handbook*. Chicago: Moody Press, 1975. 185).

While there wasn't anything romantic about the smelly, shoe-exchange in verses 1-8, the speech that Boaz made after the transaction demonstrated that he was excited, proud, and more than eager to fulfill this role. He spoke not only to the ten elders but to "all the people (4:9)." He wasn't ashamed to tell everyone exactly what he had done; in fact, he wanted them to know. He proclaimed every detail of what this transaction meant for Naomi, for Ruth, and for himself. For his part, he spent his own money in a selfless act, whereby he gave up his first child's name and inheritance to the memory and lineage of another man. For Naomi, he redeemed her inheritance, providing for her future, and rescuing her from poverty. For Ruth, he rescued her from a nameless, childless situation through his willingness to "perpetuate the name of the dead in his inheritance . . . that it may not be cut off (4:10)."

Maybe he made this public announcement because he wanted to prevent any misinterpretation of his motives. He wanted people to know that he sought this out and eagerly made this decision. He wanted no pity and no judgment. Maybe he made this show to protect Ruth, as a foreigner, from unwanted speculation that she was a gold digger or

> *At the very least, between the lines his speech screams, "Yes, I've sacrificed my own name and inheritance, but I wanted to do it!"*

> *They used the ancient name for Bethlehem, Ephrathah, thus foreshadowing the importance of that town as the birthplace of the Messiah, our willing and perfect Kinsman Redeemer.*

worse. At the very least, between the lines his speech screams, "Yes, I've sacrificed my own name and inheritance, but I wanted to do it!"

The town responded with approval. They pronounced a blessing on the union between Boaz and Ruth. They used ancestral names like Rachel, Leah, Judah, Tamar, and Perez, emphasizing the significance of their future offspring. They used the ancient name for Bethlehem, Ephrathah, thus foreshadowing the importance of that town as the birthplace of the Messiah, our willing and perfect kinsman redeemer (Micah 5:2). This blessing was pregnant with prophetic meaning as are the remaining verses in this book. But before we examine those treasures tomorrow, let's ponder some remaining applications from our verses today.

Day 11

Food for Thought Have you ever bought your spouse, your children, or a friend something very special that took much thought and sacrifice? When they received it, did they go on and on about how great the gift was, how they couldn't wait to use it or wear it, how excited they were to have it but never once stopped to acknowledge you? The fact that it came from you didn't matter at all—they were just glad they had the "thing." How did that make you feel?

Put yourself in Ruth and Naomi's sandals for a moment. What do you think some of their emotions were after this selfless, generous act by Boaz? Relief? Rejoicing? Gratitude? Think of the last time someone graciously blessed you by providing you with something that you desperately needed. Or, think of someone who gave you a generous gift. What were your emotions afterward? Surely, gratitude was high on the list. But be honest, were you more grateful for the gift or for the giver, for the provision or for the provider?

If we're not careful, this can happen in our relationship with Christ. We should rightly overflow with gratitude for all that we receive in Christ. Blessings come to us from his hand every day. But let's also remember to love and appreciate the giver. Christ alone should satisfy our hearts, not just the blessings he bestows.

Faith in Action Read Deuteronomy 23:3-6. The law of Moses proclaimed that "No . . . Moabite may enter the assembly of the LORD. Even to the tenth generation . . . forever." Thus, the law made it virtually impossible for Ruth to be saved. Her unwilling kinsman redeemer symbolized the law; he had the opportunity to redeem both her and the land, but he could not. "The law could only keep Ruth out, much less bring her in (Unger's, p. 184)." The law said, "No," because of who she was. Because of the love and grace of her willing, kinsman redeemer, however, God said, "Yes!" Likewise, because we are sinners, without the slightest ability to keep the law perfectly, we cannot enter into a relationship with God on our own (Gal 2:16). Instead, "Christ redeemed us from the curse of the law by becoming a curse for us (Gal 3:13a)." Hallelujah! Read Ephesians 1:3-14 to be reminded of all you have through your redemption in Christ.

Prayer

For your prayer today, take the words of Ephesians 1:3-14 and make them a personal prayer of thanksgiving for all of the gifts of grace, but especially for the Giver.

Day 12

Ruth 4:13–22

Who doesn't love a happy ending? We even expect them in our fairy tales. From the opening lines, "Once upon a time," we anticipate the final words, "And they lived happily ever after"—no matter the life-threatening conflicts, all-powerful opposition, or insurmountable obstacles faced.

This happy ending is no fairy tale, however; it's a true story. It's a story with a true "damsel in distress," a selfless, foreign "heroine," and a "knight in shining armor." Boaz saved the day, made the daring rescue, and married the girl he loved. In doing so, he remains one of the few men in Scripture that receives no mention of his character flaws. He was a true hero in every sense of the word.

Verse 13 of chapter 4 summarizes some major events in just a few words. Boaz took Ruth. They got married. They became lovers. God gave them a son. If we're not careful, we can skim through these "happily ever after" words and miss something big. Let's pause for a moment to remember that Ruth was married to Mahlon, and they didn't conceive a child. It wasn't because they used birth control. Something wasn't right. Perhaps Boaz had wondered about this too, which made his selfless desire to redeem her even more beautiful. Hence, the words, "The LORD gave her conception." Pause to consider and acknowledge the picture of Providence once again in this story. God himself pronounced a blessing on this demonstration of redemption with the gift of a child.

> *God himself pronounced a blessing on this demonstration of redemption with the gift of a child.*

And the pronouncements kept coming. The women of the town spoke a blessing over Naomi. They correctly directed the glory to God, who was the one who provided the redeemer for her. They identified the child as the kinsman redeemer, because he was the one who was the realized demonstration of the redemption. They called the child a "restorer of life and a nourisher (4:15)." The literal Hebrew translation means "he who causes life to return," which reversed Naomi's lament in 1:21, "the LORD . . . brought me back empty (ESV Study Bible, 483)." That's what redemption does—returns life to dead things and turns emptiness into fullness.

Ruth received high praise as well when she was described as being better to Naomi than seven sons. In light of the importance of sons in the Old Testament, this was the highest of compliments. Ruth's faithful love for Naomi continued to shine to the very end of this story. She even allowed Naomi to be the nurse and guardian to her son, Obed (4:16). This is a testimony to the fact that where mutual love, respect, and selflessness are present, even the most potentially troublesome relationships can be successful and bring glory to God.

The Book of Ruth closes with a genealogy. Instead of lifting a hand to our mouths to stifle a yawn of disinterest, we should lift our hands to worship the God who is sovereign over all—even genealogies. This important genealogy may be the reason that the Book of Ruth was included in the canon of Scripture. It's both prophetic and profound in light of the gospel. It is the genealogy of the greatest king in all of Israel, and therefore, a part of the genealogy of the

> *This important genealogy may be the reason that the Book of Ruth was included in the canon of Scripture.*

Day 12

promised Messiah—the redeemer of Israel and all of mankind.

To understand the prophetic importance of this genealogy, we must go all the way back to the Garden of Eden. Yes, the place where God created man and woman for the divine purpose of bringing him glory through a personal relationship with him. Of course, we all know what happened under that tree. Adam, Eve, the serpent, the disobedience, the broken fellowship, and the separation from God. The holy Creator couldn't let sin go unpunished, so he meted out the consequences for all involved. Genesis 3:14-19 outlines these consequences for Adam, Eve, and the serpent. But tucked away in this ugly list of curses is a whispered promise that God already had a redemption plan in place.

In Genesis 3:15, God spoke to the serpent, which had become a mouthpiece for evil, the origins of which are always Satan. God said to the serpent, "I will put enmity between you and the woman, and between your offspring [Hb. *seed*] and her offspring; he shall bruise your head, and you shall bruise his heel." This verse is widely understood as the first prophetic announcement of the Messiah. The seed of the woman (Jesus Christ, born of the virgin Mary) would be the one to redeem mankind from the consequences and curses of our sin.

In his sovereignty, God promised to do something miraculous. Through a line of sinful human beings, he would provide someone who would redeem his most cherished creation—mankind. Through him, God would reclaim humanity to enjoy his glory forever as worshipers. From this point on in Scripture, we see God preserving the ordained seed until his promise was fulfilled through the incarnation of Jesus Christ. God highlighted more details about this plan

> *From this point on in Scripture, we see God preserving the ordained seed until his promise was fulfilled through the incarnation of Jesus Christ.*

> *The forces of evil have attempted to thwart and nullify God's covenant promises throughout history, but when God makes a promise, he keeps it!*

through the specific covenants he made with Noah, Abraham, and David.

He preserved Noah through the flood and made promises "for all future generations (Gen 9:8-17)." God narrowed it down when he made a covenant with Abraham to make a "great nation" from his seed and to bless "all the families of the earth" through him (Gen 12:1-3; 17:1-8). This was the prophecy that revealed the redeemer would come through the seed of Abraham—the nation of Israel. Finally, God got very specific when he made his covenant with David (2 Sam 7:13-16). God promised that King David's line, the tribe of Judah, would produce the seed from which the Messiah would come. The stories of the Old Testament illustrate how God preserved the promised seed over and over again, by saving Noah, creating the nation of Israel, and preserving the line of Judah, the household of David. The forces of evil have attempted to thwart and nullify God's covenant promises throughout history, but when God makes a promise, he keeps it!

Day 12

Food for Thought Have you gotten the gist by now that God is not just in the "big picture" stuff, but he is in all the small details as well? He purposed that his only son would be born into the lineage of people that included a Moabitess—the converted, pagan-god worshiper, Ruth. He could've picked a more "suitable" girl to be the ancestral grandmother of David and ultimately the Messiah. But then again, the genealogy of Christ is littered with unlikely people, some who are named in our text today (check out Tamar the Canaanite and Judah in Genesis 38—that's a dousy!). How does this fact make you feel? What does this tell you about God?

Faith in Action Read the genealogy of Jesus Christ through Mary in Matthew 1:1-16. Then, read the genealogy of Christ through Joseph in Luke 3:23-38. Come on, you can do it. For fun, try to read the names out loud. Make note of any names that you see that are also in the genealogy in our text today. Do you recognize the names of any unlikely people?

According to Matthew 1:5, who was Boaz' mother? Do you think this had anything to do with Boaz' willingness to love a foreigner? It's amazing how God prepared the way for his plan to put Boaz and Ruth together, even before Boaz was born. You've studied how this story clearly and beautifully illustrates that the sovereign hand of God is at work to accomplish his purposes and fulfill his promises. Do you still doubt that he is doing that for you today?

Prayer

Sovereign God, I echo the words of Job 42:2, "I know that you can do all things, and that no purpose of yours can be thwarted." Thank you for the story in the Book of Ruth that reminds me of this. Thank you for the reminder today that your purposes and plans include unlikely people—people like me. Give me faith to believe, and spiritual eyes to see that you are at work in my life to fulfill your purposes for me (Ps 138:8).

Day 13

Reflections on the Book of Ruth

    I recently returned from a trip to Spain with my daughter. We spent three glorious weeks traveling around this beautiful country. We walked the streets of Madrid, Burgos, Leincres, Bilboa, and Valencia. We found out that you can't really experience a city unless you have walked its streets, smelled its aromas, tasted food the locals eat, attempted to speak the language, and tried to navigate its public transportation systems. While we enjoyed this adventure, one of our favorite things to do was to climb to the tallest vantage point and get a "birds-eye view" of a place. This provided us with breath-taking vistas and perspective on the size and scope of a place. It gave us another way to appreciate what we had experienced.

    Today, we will step out of the experience of Ruth's narrative, and we will seek the view from a higher vantage point—to gain a greater appreciation for what we have seen in the barley fields and at the town gate of Bethlehem. We will reflect on some extra-biblical thoughts and applications. In other words, today's devotion will all be "Food for Thought" and "Faith in Action." We'll look at some interesting things that stand out in the landscape of the story. Enjoy the view!

    Let's take another look at the characters of the story. What did you learn from them? Take a moment to write

> *Without the personal investment that Naomi made in her life, Ruth would've been back in Moab with Orpah—forgotten and lost.*

down a particular trait of each character you would like to emulate:

• Naomi

• Ruth

• Boaz

Consider Naomi—some say that she was the true "main character" of the story. The quantity of her dialogue outnumbered that of Ruth's. The story was about her family, not Ruth's. True, Ruth was the specific person that God used to accomplish his preservation of the seed in the line of David. But, there is no Ruth without Naomi. Without the personal investment that Naomi made in her life, Ruth would've been back in Moab with Orpah—forgotten and lost. Naomi added significance and value to this narrative.

Naomi was an older woman, and yet she was greatly used by God. The difficult circumstances of her life could've caused her to shut down and retreat in defeat and isolation. But she poured her life and her faith into Ruth. Her connection and investment in Ruth's life made all the difference in Ruth and Boaz's life together. And, her investment had eternal returns as well. She was blessed to play a significant role in the genealogy of the Messiah.

Have you ever used your age as an excuse to abandon God and what he is doing in your world? Have you ever thought, "I'm too young to go on this mission trip." Or, "I don't have enough experience to be involved in that ministry. I'll wait until I'm older to get involved." If you're older, maybe you've thought, "I'm too old, no one will value what I have to offer." Or, "I've done my time in ministry. I'm tired. It's time for me to just relax." Remember, you are never too young or too old to make an eternal investment in the life of someone else—just like Naomi did.

Day 13

When you pour your faith, your care, and your life into another person, there will always be eternal returns.

Who are you spiritually investing in right now? Read Philippians 1:20-26. The Apostle Paul was determined to be used by God in the lives of others until the very end of his life. Pray right now and ask God to show you how you can invest in the spiritual lives of others for his glory.

Next, consider Ruth—she was the willing responder to Naomi's actions. Because she was teachable and humble, she valued Naomi. Ruth was willing, obedient, and hardworking. These traits are hard to find in people today—especially those who are young like Ruth. God uses all types of vessels for his kingdom purposes: age is irrelevant, looks don't matter, ethnicity is not a criterion, socio-economic status is meaningless, a certain level of spiritual maturity isn't even required. The thing that really matters is willing obedience. God uses willing vessels!

Matthew 25:14-30 records the parable of the talents. Three slaves were given some money to manage by their master. The clear expectation was that they would invest it for a profitable gain. Three different amounts were given—only one expectation. Two of the slaves willingly followed the wishes of their master. The third had his own idea about what was best and did his own thing. In the time of reckoning, the only thing that mattered to the master was that his slaves did what he wanted them to do. The amount of the profit didn't matter, only that they fulfilled their purpose. The two obedient slaves with differing gains were given the same reward, "Well done, good and faithful slave! You were faithful over a few things; I will put you in charge of many things. Share your master's joy (25: 21, 23)!" Sadly, the third slave was unwilling to obey the master and lost the opportunity to experience his favor (25:24-29).

Remember, you are never too young or too old to make an eternal investment in the life of someone else.

How does this illustration given by Jesus encourage you? How does it challenge you? Pray

> *God uses all types of vessels for his kingdom purposes: age is irrelevant, looks don't matter, ethnicity is not a criterion, socio-economic status is meaningless, a certain level of spiritual maturity isn't even required. The thing that really matters is willing obedience.*

and ask God to forgive where you have fought against his purposes in order to get your own way. Then, ask him to help you to be a "good and faithful" servant. Give yourself to him as a willing vessel for him to use as he purposes today.

Then, consider Boaz—when you take a look from above, he looks a lot like Jesus, doesn't he? The ESV Study Bible states that he "prefigures Christ." What do you think that means? If you can't remember, go back and review Day 8.

Finally, consider redemption—it's the major theme of this book. Merriam Webster's simple definition of the word *redeem* is to "make better or more acceptable (something that is bad, unpleasant, etc.)". The full definition is "to free from what distresses or harms (ransom, extricate, release, free from)."

Naomi and Ruth were both beneficiaries of redemption. Naomi was freed from poverty, anonymity, emptiness, and bitterness (1:20-21). Chapter 4:14-15 described her new status as restored, nourished, and loved. She was made better and freed from bad and unpleasant distresses—REDEEMED!

Ruth was extricated from godless idolatry and became a fearer of YAHWEH, the God of Israel (1:16). Her unpleasant status as a "servant" (2:13-Hb. *shipkhah* meaning slave-servant) with limited rights, changed to "servant" (3:9-Hb. *'amah* meaning maidservant) with the right to enjoy the privileges of an Israelite house-

> *A life without Christ is a life without hope. But his death on the cross provided redemption, ransoming us from a life apart from God, freeing us to live abundantly in him.*

Day 13

hold, including giving birth to an heir (ESV Study Bible, 480-481). She was released from being a childless widow and made a "daughter (2:2)," a wife, and mother (4:10, 13)—REDEEMED!

We are all sinners in desperate need of a Savior and a Redeemer. Without a Savior, we would die in our sins and spend an eternity separated from God in hell. Without a Redeemer, we would still be enslaved to our wicked hearts, unable to free ourselves from the power of sin. A life without Christ is a life without hope. But his death on the cross provided redemption, ransoming us from a life apart from God, freeing us to live abundantly in him (Jn 10:10).

If you are a believer, you are "in Christ." Read Ephesians 1:3-11 again and be reminded of all that is yours because you are redeemed. Spend some time thanking God for all your spiritual blessings. Worship him and give him glory.

The view from above is pretty amazing!

Day 14

Introduction to Esther

Now, it's Esther's turn to tell us her story. If we could sit with her, it wouldn't be in the village coffee shop; it would be in an opulent palace sitting room, sipping tea. Undoubtedly, we would be a little nervous trying to mind our "p's and q's". In spite of her royalty, Queen Esther's likeability would put us at ease as we posed our questions. While we may want to jump to the "good stuff," she would want us to start at the beginning and get the whole story. So, get a good handle on that dainty tea cup so you won't stain that one-of-a-kind Persian rug, and listen carefully. There are many things in her story that won't make sense unless we understand the prelude. We need to know where she came from to fully appreciate where she ends up.

In 586 BC, about a hundred years before Esther became queen, the Babylonian Empire took her ancestors captive. This forced captivity was an act of God's judgment on his people for their continued disobedience and idolatry. However, by God's grace, the Jews not only survived their exile, but also thrived in spite of it. Cyrus of Persia conquered Babylon and put an end to the Jewish Babylonian captivity in 539 BC, in fulfillment of biblical prophecy in Isaiah 44:28 and 45:1, 13. Not all Jews returned to their homeland, though. Many remained in the cities where they had established a life. Esther's ancestors were among those who chose to stay.

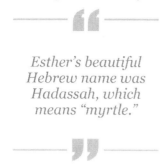

Esther's beautiful Hebrew name was Hadassah, which means "myrtle."

Cyrus reigned for approximately nine years (539-530 BC); Darius the Mede ruled the kingdom next (521-486 BC); and then Darius' son, Ahasuerus, took the throne (486-465 BC). The Old Testament books of Ezra and Nehemiah focus on the activities of the first group of Jewish people who returned to Jerusalem. Nehemiah led a group back from exile under King Cyrus to rebuild the city walls. Ezra led a second group of exiles back to Jerusalem around 458 BC under King Artaxerxes (Ahasuerus' son) to finish rebuilding the temple—the work laid dormant for 17 years! This group is documented in Ezra 7-10. The events in the Book of Esther took place from 483 to 473 BC, while Ahasuerus was king, and it focuses on what happened to the Jewish families who chose to remain in Babylon.

Only Ezra 7-10, Nehemiah, and Malachi record history later than the Book of Esther. The Old Testament ends with the Persian Empire in control. The Greek Empire rose during the 400 years when there were no prophets in Israel, and God seemed to be silent. The Roman Empire followed the Greeks, and then God spoke loudly when the "Word became flesh and dwelt among us (Jn 1:14)." The Son of God, our Immanuel, entered our world under Roman rule.

Esther's beautiful Hebrew name was Hadassah, which means "myrtle." Her father, who is mentioned twice, was Abihail (2:15; 9:29). At some point, Esther's father and mother both died, and her older cousin, Mordecai, took her in. He became like a father to her. They lived in Susa, one of the four capital cities of the Persian Empire. We can only imagine the impact on Esther's life being raised without a mother. She missed the valuable love and nurture that a mother brings to every girl. However, because a man raised her, she probably possessed a stronger comfort level around men, which probably helped her "find favor" with Hegai (2:8) and ultimately the king. Isn't it amazing

Day 14

how God works! God uses our biggest losses to strengthen us for the life circumstances he knows we'll face.

We aren't sure who wrote Esther's story. Some commentators suggest Ezra, Nehemiah, or men of the Great Synagogue (EBC, Vol. 4, 777). Most say that it had to be a Persian Jew, who had knowledge and familiarity with Persian customs and the palace itself. It is written as a narrative and is included in the section of the Hebrew Bible called "the Writings;" this includes everything except the Torah and the Prophets. It is the last of the "megilloths," or the five scrolls, and it's read at the final Jewish festival of the year, the Feast of Purim. Many Jews would agree that it is one of the most popular books in the Old Testament, and it's still read in its entirety every year in synagogues and Jewish faith communities.

John MacArthur compares the events in the Book of Esther to "a chess game played by God and Satan (MBC, 554)." Ever since God created man in his own image, Satan has jealously attempted to destroy God's relationship with mankind. His priority has also been to keep God from fulfilling his covenant promises with the nation of Israel. Satan's relentless mission is revealed in vivid and violent colors throughout the events in Esther's story. This "chess match" finds both God and Satan moving real kings, queens, and nobles. When Satan put Haman in place he declared, "Check." God then positioned Esther and Mordecai with an emphatic "Checkmate!" The imagery of God as the chess Grandmaster, who anticipated every move of his opponent, is fascinating and should inspire our confidence to trust in him with every detail of our lives.

One question we might ask Esther would be in regard to the depth of her personal faith in God. There is no mention of God in this entire book, so some have speculated that neither Mordecai nor Esther possessed a strong faith. Wouldn't it be great if Esther herself could confirm or deny this?

God uses our biggest losses to strengthen us for the life circumstances he knows we'll face.

87

> *God uses trials to cause us to acknowledge our need for his divine help.*

Perhaps she would tell us that the unusual and life-threatening circumstances of her life caused her faith to grow as she navigated them, especially when she could do nothing else but rely on the providential hand of God to intervene. We can relate, can't we? God uses the trials of our lives to cause us to look to him, lean on him, cry out to him, and acknowledge our own need for his divine help. That's why James 1:2-3 tells us to "count it all joy, my brothers, when you meet trials of various kinds, for you know that the testing of your faith produces steadfastness."

Narratives don't always give us interesting information, such as how a person feels or what they were thinking in certain circumstances. So, we would definitely want to ask Esther what she was thinking when she was taken away to the palace for her own personal Persian version of "The Bachelor." Did she truly fall in love with the king? Did he ever really love her? What about the other women? Did they hate her because she was beautiful and favored? How hard was it to keep her identity a secret? What did it feel like to have the weight of her people's very existence on her exquisitely, delicate shoulders?

Biblical scholars, historians, moviemakers, and interested readers have attempted to read between the lines and come up with their own opinions and answers about these questions. Scripture tells us what happened—just the facts. Period. But there is sufficient detail to know that God supernaturally intervened in the course of history to protect the nation of Israel from being destroyed, so that his prophesied plan of redemption for all of mankind could be completed. We

> *God supernaturally intervened in the course of history to protect the nation of Israel from being destroyed, so that his prophesied plan of redemption for all of mankind could be completed.*

Day 14

will stay true to the biblical narrative during our study, but we'll explore some of the possibilities hidden between the lines.

Esther is a famous woman of the Bible. Her name is mentioned 55 times, while Abraham's Sarah is only mentioned 51 (Edith Deen, *All of the Women of the Bible*, 147). Her name has been immortalized in art tapestries at Windsor Castle in the Queen's Audience Chamber. The French dramatist, Jean Racinethat, wrote a three-act play based on her life in 1689. And George Frideric Handel wrote an oratorio called "The Sacred Story of Esther" in 1732. Her story has fascinated people for centuries. No doubt we will leave our time with her knowing that Esther truly was an instrument of God—an ordinary, orphan girl put into a powerful position by an extraordinary and all-powerful God; the one whose business it is to save, redeem, and make his name glorious. That's what God does—he delights to use his image-bearers to accomplish his purposes, but without exception, he always desires and deserves to get the glory for who he is and what he does!

> *Esther truly was an instrument of God—an ordinary, orphan girl put into a powerful position by an extraordinary and all-powerful God; the one whose business it is to save, redeem, and make his name glorious.*

Food for Thought Why do you think the author of Esther did not put God's name in the narrative (Song of Solomon is the only other book in the Bible that doesn't mention God's name)? Maybe it's because the excitement of discovery is heightened by the challenge of the search. Think of the appeal of picture search games like "Where's Waldo?" or the fun of a treasure hunt. Or, consider the pictures filled with colorful shapes, which upon further concentration reveal fascinating new scenes. The Book of Esther is like that. Discovering God's hand at work through the story will be exciting and reassuring. Just like the aforementioned puzzles, once you discover the "hidden" picture, you'll see it more clearly every time you look.

Faith in Action Read the entire Book of Esther to become familiar with it before we dive into deeper waters tomorrow. We'll snorkel today, and start scuba diving tomorrow. If you've ever done both of these things, you know the difference between seeing things from the surface as opposed to being up close and personal. Ask God to begin to reveal the hidden shadows of his sovereignty as you read.

Prayer Heavenly Father, reveal yourself to me as I study the Book of Esther. Don't let me miss you just because your name isn't mentioned. Help me to see your eternal purposes as you work through the lives of kings, queens, and ordinary people like Mordecai, Esther and me.

Day 15

Esther 1:1–9

The setting for our story centers around the Persian palace at Susa. To really immerse yourself in the story, picture in your mind the last palace you visited, or read about, or wished you had visited, or just Googled. (That's right, go ahead and Google "royal palaces" if necessary.) Look at the pictures and read a little of the history. You will discover that most palaces were built for one very important reason—to show off wealth, power, and position. They are a more grandiose demonstration of the modern-day idea that "he who has the most toys wins!"

One such palace is Neuschwanstein Castle in Germany. It is aptly nicknamed the "castle of the fairy tale king." In fact, Walt Disney fashioned his iconic castle at Disneyland after this very palace. Ludwig II, king of Bavaria, built Neuschwanstein for his personal dwelling and designed it as a monument of sorts to his love of the arts, music, and theater. The growing kingdom of Prussia had rendered Bavaria powerless and its king ineffective. So Ludwig II spent his personal fortune to build an opulent palace where he could still imagine himself as a powerful ruler, surrounded by all of the things that made him feel like a king. I was able to visit this impressive castle in the summer of 2014 and was awestruck by the extravagance of each magnificent ballroom, luxurious bedroom, and palatial corridor. Ludwig went all out trying to make a statement that he was still king. He had money, and he wasn't going to let another king take that lifestyle from him.

> *He was a typical emperor—power hungry, strong, indifferent, cruel, and sexually immoral.*

The same is true about the palace in Susa. In fact, the Medo-Persian Empire was so vast that it had four capital cities. The empire reached from India to Ethiopia. Royalty spent the winters in Susa, so many of the customs were probably duplicated in the other three capitals, including palaces, harems, and wives.

A man named Herodotus is called "the father of history." He documented this era in "Histories," his book about the Greco-Persian wars. It was published in 440 BC and was one of the first history books in . . . well, history. The Expositor's Bible Commentary references information from this book, especially because it talks about specific people, places, and events in our story. We'll find out some interesting tidbits from Herodotus along the way.

The time was 483 BC, three years after Ahasuerus had become King of the Medo-Persian Empire. He was a warrior king, because he rose to power after quelling uprisings in Egypt and Babylon (EBC, 798). From all descriptions, he was a typical emperor—power hungry, strong, indifferent, cruel, and sexually immoral. He was so obsessed with conquering Greece that he threw a six-month-long party (aka a political, fund-raising event) just to strategize and gain support for his political and military aspirations. And, well, to show off a little.

He invited nobles, military leaders, political leaders, and everybody who was anybody from all over the empire to this party. The Bible says he even included their servants (1:3). Realistically, it was probably a big "drop in," where the invited guests came in rotation, staying for a time until the next group arrived. However, as many as 15,000 guests were entertained at once at some Persian banquets, and one King of Assyria was reported to have entertained almost 70,000 guests for 10 days (EBC, 798). Whatever the logistics were, it was one BIG event!

Day 15

At the end of the six months, the king threw one final party that lasted for seven days. This guest list included "all the people present in Susa the citadel, both great and small (1:5)." This special feast took place in the courtyard garden of the palace. We have no idea how many were at this feast, but we do know that it was a garden full of men with an open bar and no "cut offs" for drinking (1:8). One can only imagine the level of drunkenness and testosterone at this banquet.

The detailed description in verse 6 of the opulent room and furnishings has been verified by archaeological findings of the remains of this very palace (EBC, 799). The fact that wine was served in gold vessels of all different kinds may refer to some of the vessels that were taken as spoils from the temple at Jerusalem by Nebuchadnezzar in 587 BC (EBC, 799).

At the same time, Queen Vashti was throwing a feast of her own for the women. Let's pause and reflect on Vashti for a moment. First and foremost, she was stunningly beautiful. The Persian Empire, like many countries today, was obsessed with beauty and sexuality. Queen Vashti would definitely have made the covers of Vogue, Cosmopolitan, and Glamour, including articles about her suggested beauty tips, skincare regimens, and workout routines.

As they say, beauty is only skin-deep, and that was definitely true of Vashti. Greek literature recorded that she was Amestris of history, who was cruel, arrogant, and domineering (EBC, 789)—think Cinderella's wicked step-mother. She must have been married to Ahasuerus for some time, and they had two sons prior to his ascent to the throne. Her third son, Artaxerxes, was born in 483 BC; the same year that our story begins. Interestingly, she may have been either pregnant or a new mother at the time of the big party. Artaxerxes became king (Ezra 7:1) after Aha-

Beauty is only skin-deep, and that was definitely true of Vashti.

We are to give worth to people based on who they are as image-bearers of God.

suerus was murdered in 465 BC by the eunuchs who guarded his royal bedchamber. So, she was later a queen mother as well.

Two banquets . . . the seventh day . . . testosterone and estrogen levels sky high . . . and then, it all hit the fan. God's first sovereign move was made to vacate the position of queen. The scene is set, and we know King Ahasuerus and Queen Vashti a little better. Get ready for some intrigue.

Day 15

Food for Thought

We live in a materialistic culture in many ways like the Persian Empire. We erroneously judge people based on what they possess or what they don't possess. We assign worth to those who have nice things (i.e. cars, big houses, name-brand handbags, expensive watches, the latest technology, etc.) and devalue those who have very little. This could be called socio-economic prejudice.

We also assign undue worth to those who are physically attractive, based on that fact alone. Why do we believe that we can look like someone else by using the same products they use? And why do we seem to be mesmerized by beautiful people as if they possess something worthy of our admiration solely on their outward appearance. Are they smarter because they're beautiful? No. Can they make a difference in the world based on their physical appearance? No. Do they influence people for good because they are good looking? No. Does God use them more? Absolutely not! Both of these demonstrate misplaced favor. Instead, we are to give worth to people based on who they are as image-bearers of God. We are to give worth to possessions only as potential objects for bringing God glory.

Faith in Action

How would you know if you participate in this kind of prejudice of assigning misplaced worth? Ask yourself the following questions and be honest: Are you enamored with the above-mentioned status symbols? Do you find yourself wanting more things or thinking your life would be better if you HAD a particular thing? Do you ever find yourself "bragging" about what you have? Do you "feel sorry" for people who don't have what you have? Do you tend to favor those with money over those with *very little? Do you find yourself idolizing or admiring someone based solely on his or her appearance? Read James 2:1-4 and use the given scenario to take a "test" on whether you "show partiality" or not.*

Prayer

Father in heaven, forgive me for falling prey to these cultural tendencies. I repent of my tendency to desire and pursue the things that this world values. Help me to value people based on the fact that they are your image-bearers. And teach me to value my possessions only as they can be used for your kingdom to bring you glory.

Day 16

Esther 1:10–22

King Ahasuerus and Queen Vashti had both reached critical moments. A drunk, egotistical King Ahasuerus, his ability to think clearly diminished, was spurred onto idiocy and thoughtless bravado by the other drunk, egotistical men at the banquet. Even when alcohol is not involved, a golf outing or hunting trip with a group of guys can quickly turn into a comparison of physical or financial "muscles," or a discussion about who has the biggest shrew for a wife. Since this whole thing was about showing off, King Ahasuerus had one more thing to show off—his wife. In case anyone doubted that he had it all, he "commanded" his eunuchs to "bring Queen Vashti" to "show . . . her beauty (1:10-11)." Considering the drunken and debauched state of the king and his guests, we can safely assume that this demand was motivated by the desire for sinful sexuality. One can only imagine the lewd comments that were flying in anticipation of the queen's arrival.

This command—not request—was relayed to the queen by not one, but all seven of the king's personal eunuchs. One of them definitely drew the short straw when they decided which one would speak. The other six lended their support, or protection, or both. After all, they were going into a room full of "sisters," who were involved in their own "girl's night out"—think bachelorette party in Las Vegas. As is often the case on these occasions, a full-on diva competition was being played out, where men bashing was the main agenda. They were probably dis-

> *In our culture today, women are too often seen as sexual objects to be used rather than as people to be valued.*

cussing whose husband was the most insensitive jerk. "Girl power" was on full display! We can imagine the combined gasp by all the women at the demand made by the nervous eunuch; a gasp that was strong enough to suck all of the air out of the room.

Queen Vashti did not politely decline but "refused to come at the king's command (1:12)." The reason for her refusal is not given, but it could've been for several reasons. First, she probably knew that if she was paraded in front of a group of drunken men, it would illicit lewd and degrading responses. She would be like a piece of meat on display. Second, she could've been pregnant with Artaxerxes (MBC, 556). If he was just an infant, maybe she had not regained her pre-birth figure yet. Or third, she had no desire to obey her husband or to be flaunted as his trophy. If she was the imperious Amestris, she probably felt no inclination to obey her husband's impetuous whim, much less respectfully decline.

While we should neither admire nor imitate Queen Vashti, at least in this instance she didn't allow herself to become a sexual object. Whatever her motives, she chose not to bow to the pressure to flaunt her looks. In our culture today, women are too often seen as sexual objects to be used rather than as people to be valued. We should remember that women are image-bearers of God and, like men, should be treated with equal value and respect.

Queen Vashti's refusal was relayed to the king, and he was furious. His ego suffered a tremendous blow—and in front of his male "friends" and subjects no less. He immediately commiserated with the "wise men who knew the times (1:13)." It was customary for the king to consult experts in matters of law and justice in order to hear their opinions. These men occupied the highest positions in the kingdom (Ezra 7:14). They were the "seven princes of Persia and Media (1:14)." Memucan was their spokesman.

Day 16

The king wanted to know what could be done to the queen for disobeying his command. Evidently, there were laws that protected a queen from the whims of a king. But this could not be! A demonstration was needed to show the people who was boss. These men had to do something

Women are image-bearers of God and, like men, should be treated with equal value and respect.

to make sure that their wives wouldn't follow the queen's example and think that they could say "No" to their husbands. Bedlam would ensue—or "contempt and wrath in plenty (1:18)." This was a national security matter! If the queen could refuse the king, what would stop all the wives of the kingdom from rebelling against their husbands? Memucan said, "Queen Vashti has not only defied the king, but she has defied every man in the kingdom (1:16)!" This is what we call a drastic overreaction.

Memucan called for dramatic action in order to ensure that Queen Vashti would be adequately punished, and women everywhere would get the message that disrespecting their husbands would not be tolerated. The first part of the decree demanded that the queen be immediately removed from her position and NEVER allowed into the king's presence again for the rest of her life. This was indeed harsh, since he was the father of her three children. Which begs the question, "Did she have to leave her infant son, Artaxerxes, at the palace when she left?" The second part of the decree was that her position as queen would be stripped from her and given to another. She was totally removed and replaced. If she was the ruthless Amestris, "The advisors wanted to be sure that Vashti could never again be restored to the king's favor, lest she take vengeance on them (EBC, 802)." Chapter 1:19 makes reference to the fact that Persian law could not be repealed (cf., 8:8 and Dan

With one drunken demand and one flat refusal, things were prepped for a divine replacement.

> *Anytime ego or disrespect go unchecked, there's potential for disastrous outcomes.*

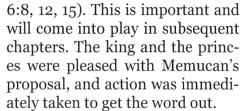

6:8, 12, 15). This is important and will come into play in subsequent chapters. The king and the princes were pleased with Memucan's proposal, and action was immediately taken to get the word out.

Letters were written and sent to "*every* province," and "*every* people," and they proclaimed that "*every* man" be the master of his household (emphasis mine—note all the times that "every" is used in 1:22). The Persian mail system was reputedly excellent, and that fact is highlighted both here and later in the book. Fast horses were sent throughout the empire with kingdom edicts and laws. Soon every household knew that every man was to be "master in his own household (1:22)." And Queen Vashti was thrown out, banished, gone! With one drunken demand and one flat refusal, things were prepped for a divine replacement.

Day 16

Food for Thought

Knowing what we do about the questionable character of both King Ahasuerus and Queen Vashti, it is difficult to feel sorry for either of them, much less choose sides. There is plenty of blame and fault to go around here. Instead, we can learn from their poor examples of disrespect and selfishness, and their inability to request or respond with any sort of kindness or consideration of the other person.

If you have been a spouse for any length of time, you have hopefully figured out that demanding love, respect, or consideration from your husband or wife doesn't get you very far—nor is it biblical. If you are a husband, consider the benefits of encouraging and enabling your wife to respect you by leading with Christ-like love and servanthood. If you are a wife, consider the benefits of encouraging your husband to love you as a servant leader, by responding to him with respect and kindness—no matter the circumstance.

Lessons can be learned for everyone here in regard to how we relate to others. Rather than demanding to be treated a certain way, begin by demonstrating that attribute yourself. Like our scene from today, anytime ego or disrespect go unchecked, there's potential for disastrous outcomes.

Faith in Action

Read Luke 6:31 and Ephesians 5:15-33. Wherever you are in your spiritual journey or situation in life, what do you need to work on according to these verses? Write down what the Holy Spirit reveals to you as you read.

Prayer

Father, thank you for what you teach us in your word through both positive examples and negative examples, like those of King Ahasuerus and Queen Vashti. Show me when I am demanding, disrespectful, and inconsiderate. Fill me with your Spirit, and empty me of selfish demands and sinful desires. Enable me to submit to my Christian brothers and sisters out of reverence for Christ.

Day 17

Esther 2

About four years had passed since the events of chapter 1. During that time, King Ahasuerus left Susa with his armies to go to battle with the Persian's long-time enemy—the Greeks. History records the battle prowess of the Greeks and their unwillingness to submit to the Medo-Persian Empire. Herodotus wrote about many of their battles in his book about the Greco-Persian wars. For the war enthusiast, a mere Google search will fill your computer screen with detailed stories of some of the most famous battles in this multi-year war. Ahasuerus (whose Greek name was Xerxes) was the commanding king of the epic Battle of Thermopylae, where the Persians defeated 300 skilled and stubborn Greek warriors. They went on to get revenge by torching Athens, and they overran a large portion of Greece. King Ahasuerus was emboldened after this victory and rallied for a big battle at Salamis, where he hoped to finally squelch the Greek rebellion. Persian ships were lured into the narrow isthmus with some misleading intel. The Greeks were waiting and ready. The Persians suffered an embarrassing defeat and were forced to retreat. Ahasuerus returned to Susa, and within the year the Greeks defeated the Persians at the Battle of Plataea, thus ending their invasion of Greece. They never came under the rule of the Medo-Persian Empire.

In chapter 2:1, we find the king back in the palace—defeated, humiliated, and remembering that he had no queen. "He remembered Vashti (1:1)." Somehow the king's

> *It's interesting to note that Mordecai's name is mentioned more times in this book than Esther's, and it's important to note that he's just as prominent and significant in the story as Esther, perhaps more so.*

personal household servants understood that the king was unhappy because he had sent Vashti away. It couldn't have been simply because he missed a woman's company; he had an entire harem of women, for goodness sake. Maybe he was kicking himself for getting so carried away with the "let's show these women who's boss" demonstration. Perhaps he was contemplating a way to reinstate his beautiful, former queen. Regardless, his personal attendants rushed to get his mind on another solution. They didn't want Vashti to come back and have a chance to retaliate against them--they knew how ruthless she was.

So, they proposed a plan to the king. The plan was an elaborate one, and God's sovereign hand was all over it. Officers in all of the provinces of the kingdom were to "gather all the beautiful young virgins to the harem (1:3)," after they were "sought out" for the king (1:2). This was not a contest where volunteers lined up for the privilege of being chosen; it was a search and gather mission.

The large group of young, innocent women were to be brought to the palace and put under the "custody of Hegai (1:3)," the eunuch in charge of the king's harem. Then the women would be given beauty treatments for 12 months to prepare them for one night with the king. They were to be treated with the very best ointments and cosmetics and given a regimen of expensive skin treatments and facials. While this sounds like the kind of pampering that every woman desires, we should remember that these women were not at the palace voluntarily. They didn't have any choices here. Also, love was never part of the equation. This was a mission for the king . . . to satisfy the king sexually. . . end of story. The main criteria in choosing a queen was that she be beautiful and pleasing to the king. Outward beauty was the one and only criteria. However,

Day 17

God used this to move one beautiful woman of his choosing into place—exactly where he needed her to be.

At this point of the story (1:5-7), we are introduced to our two main characters: Mordecai and Esther. They are both Jews, living in exile in Susa, and their names are only mentioned in Scripture in this book. Let's take some time to get to know them a little better, beginning with Mordecai. Tomorrow, we will study Esther more closely.

Mordecai was a Benjamite from the tribe of Judah. His great-grandfather was taken captive when Nebuchadnezzar was king of Babylon, so he was a third-generation captive. There is no mention of a wife. The only other family member mentioned is Abihail (1:15), who was his uncle. But Mordecai's uncle and aunt died and left behind a daughter, so he took her in, raised her, and was a father to her. It's interesting to note that Mordecai's name is mentioned more times in this book than Esther's, and it's important to note that he's just as prominent and significant in the story as Esther, perhaps more so.

It's evident in this story that Mordecai loved Esther. We can only imagine the anguish he must have felt when the girl he loved like his own daughter was taken away from him to the palace, along with the other young, beautiful virgins. No more daily chats over breakfast; no more girlish laughter that brought joy to his day; no more warm smiles after a long day's work. He had no choice but to watch her leave.

He probably knew enough about the customs of the empire to be deeply concerned for her welfare and future. But he had time before she left to make one request of her; he asked her not to tell anyone that she was a Jew. This seems odd on the surface, since there were Jews everywhere in the capital. Esther was certainly not the only Jewish girl rounded up in the search for a queen. The

Mordecai must have known enough about the political temperature of the day to be concerned about the anti-Semitism bubbling below the surface of some influential Persians.

reasons are a mystery, especially since Mordecai did not keep his own nationality a secret.

>
> We can say with confidence that God kept Esther's identity veiled, because it was necessary within his sovereign plan.
>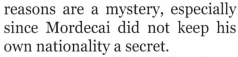

We can only speculate about the reasons behind this request. There were obviously no concerns from the palace about the nationality of the girls. The only criterion was that they be beautiful virgins. However, Mordecai must have known enough about the political temperature of the day to be concerned about the anti-Semitism bubbling below the surface of some influential Persians. He must have realized that it would be dangerous for her to be forthright with her identity. Ezra 4:6 talks about a letter written to King Ahasuerus about the Jews who had returned to Jerusalem to rebuild the walls. It was a hostile accusation against the Jews and verification that hatred for the Jewish people was alive and well in the empire.

Chapter 2:11 provides evidence that Mordecai was concerned for Esther. He went to the women's quarters and checked on her daily. The fact that he was allowed in this area of the palace means that he could've been a eunuch himself, since only eunuchs were allowed in the harems. Regardless, this choice of action seems risky. Suspicion could've been raised about Mordecai's connection to Esther. The fact that no one investigated could mean that: 1) no one cared; 2) no one noticed; or 3) there were no paparazzi in Susa. But, since people have always been nosy, none of these was the case. As a result, we can say with confidence that God kept Esther's identity veiled, because it was necessary within his sovereign plan.

Since we will talk about Esther tomorrow, let's skip ahead to the end of chapter 2 for some more information about Mordecai. In 2:21-23, we discover Mordecai's occupation. He was an appointed official who sat at the king's gate. As you remember from our story of Ruth, this was the place where the appointed elders and officials settled legal matters or disputes among the kingdom subjects. Since

Day 17

there were many Jewish people in the city, Mordecai probably handled their business.

One day while he was on the job, he overheard a conversation between two eunuchs that literally changed his life. He heard them discussing a plot to assassinate the king. As shocking as it sounds, it was not an unusual thing to try and kill the king; it happened all the time. While the king was not his favorite person either, he did the right thing and told Esther, who in turn alerted the king. The plot was investigated, uncovered, the eunuchs were hanged, and the king's life was saved.

While Mordecai's actions may have been ignored and forgotten at that moment, God knew the truth and had it recorded and filed away, ready to be used at just the right time.

The common Persian means of execution was to be "hanged on the gallows (2:23)." We may envision a hangman's noose, but it was more gruesome than that. It meant to be impaled on a large pole and left to "hang" until death (Ezra 6:11). Not a pleasant visual!

Somehow in the process of the investigation and judgment, Mordecai was not properly celebrated as the one who saved the life of the king. But God was working his plan even in this situation. There were people who got paid to write down everything that happened in palace life in a "book of the chronicles." While Mordecai's actions may have been ignored and forgotten at that moment, God knew the truth and had it recorded and filed away, ready to be used at just the right time.

30 Days to Ruth/Esther

Food for Thought

Do you find it interesting that a big part of the preparation plan for the queen contest was a 12-month beauty treatment? Cosmetics and skin care products are a huge industry and have been around since Bible times. In fact, there is a skin cream on the market today that costs around $1,000 for 1.7 ounces—as mind-boggling as that sounds (it's La Prairie Cellular Cream Platinum Rare, if you want to order some). Most of us, men and women alike, desire to be attractive to someone. We may not be willing to spend $1,000 an ounce, but we spend time and money on things that improve our looks all the time (think haircuts, mani-pedis, hair products, skin products, gym memberships, etc). While this is certainly not all bad, our priorities can become misplaced. It may even become an idol in our life. If we're not careful, we can put more effort into improving our physical bodies and neglect the most important part—our heart and soul. What would happen if we invested as much time and money into our spiritual health as we did our physical health and appearance?

Faith in Action

What kind of man do you think Mordecai was? Write down some of his character traits that you observed from your reading today. Do you wonder how Mordecai felt when no one gave him any props for saving the king's life? Can you relate? Sometimes it can seem like "no good deed goes unpunished," right? But God sees and knows everything! Read Galatians 6:9 and Colossians 3:23-24. How do these verses encourage you today? How can you apply them to a specific circumstance in your life?

Day 17

Prayer

Heavenly Father, forgive any desire or endeavor of my life that has become an idol—replacing the preeminence or importance that should be yours and yours alone. I want to live my life in a way that pleases you, not for recognition from others, but for the reward and blessing of realizing that you see, know, and are pleased when I follow and obey you.

Esther 2

Today, we study Esther—the reluctant heroine and savior of her people. But before she became God's chosen vessel of salvation, she was simply a young, ordinary, orphaned girl, living her life as an exile in a foreign land. Esther wasn't from an important family with a royal pedigree, nor did she possess a special gift or talent that made her a superstar among her peers. She was just a girl.

She was introduced as Hadassah, her Jewish name. But every Jewish exile received a pagan name, and hers was Esther. When we meet her in the pages of Scripture, she was old enough to be married—at least a teenager. She had only an adoptive father, and he was her cousin—the only family she had. She probably lived a simple life, took care of her "father," and did what all young Jewish girls did.

The Bible says she "had a beautiful figure and was lovely to look at (2:7)." The HCSB says she had a "beautiful figure and was extremely good-looking." While the NASB says she was "beautiful of form and face." We get the picture—she was gorgeous! So, of course, she was "gathered" and "taken" to the palace with all the other "beautiful, young virgins (2:2)."

Josephus said that there were as many as 400 girls gathered and taken to the palace (EBC, 806). It's hard to visualize or analyze this scene accurately. We can guess that some went kicking and screaming, afraid and sad to leave loved ones, friends, and the familiar. Some may have

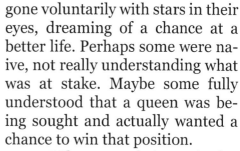

> *Esther wasn't from an important family with a royal pedigree, nor did she possess a special gift or talent that made her a superstar among her peers. She was just a girl.*

gone voluntarily with stars in their eyes, dreaming of a chance at a better life. Perhaps some were naive, not really understanding what was at stake. Maybe some fully understood that a queen was being sought and actually wanted a chance to win that position.

Whatever their attitudes may have been, they weren't really given a choice. If they were "beautiful, young virgins," they were gathered and taken to the palace and put in the "custody" of Hegai. This word alone implies that the women weren't free to come and go as they wished.

We can only imagine the fear that Esther must have experienced during her capture. She did make several key choices throughout this situation, though. She chose to listen to Mordecai's request and not tell anyone that she was a Jew. She trusted him and did what he said. She also chose to submit to the circumstance in a way that impressed Hegai. She "pleased him and won his favor (2:9)." Maybe it was her attitude, demeanor, or personality. It had to be something besides her outward beauty, because she was there with hundreds of beautiful girls. We understand that certain inward qualities can magnify outward beauty—humility, authenticity, quiet confidence, warmth, kindness, or grace. We can only piece together a theory about which of these qualities made Esther stand out. Let's not forget that the main reason she won favor with Hegai was that God was sovereignly moving her into the place she needed to be. But God used who she was, and she did stand out among all the young ladies.

Since Hegai singled her out as a frontrunner, her beauty regimen and special diet was started "quickly". She was personally given seven young servants who were hand-picked from the king's palace, and she was "advanced" to the best rooms in the harem (2:9). Given Hegai's position

Day 18

and experience, he most likely had a keen instinct about which girls would be potential queen material.

The process took a whole year (by the way, any man who complains about his wife or girlfriend taking too long to get ready should be glad it doesn't take a year). First, there were six months of oil of myrrh treatments. This valued, essential oil is still used today. While it is most commonly used for skin health, it also has other medicinal properties. It has anti-infection, anti-fungal and anti-inflammatory properties. It was historically used to treat cancer, leprosy, syphilis, and herpes (Modern Essentials, Sixth Ed., 119). In other words, they wanted their candidates beautiful and disease free—no wrinkles, no skin imperfections, and no infections.

Then there were six months of "spices and ointments (2:12)." This probably meant perfumes, cosmetics, mud baths, and further skin treatments with all the other essential oils in use at that time. At any rate, they were serious about covering all the beauty bases.

Life during this year was full of "regulations for the women." While this was by no means torture for the women, it was a life void of independence. The strict regulations were not abusive, but they were restrictive. From the moment that they were selected, their lives changed forever. They were away from family and home. Their lives were scheduled and regulated. There was almost no chance for love and children of their own. They were essentially healthy, sweet-smelling sex slaves, with soft, beautiful skin, who were prepped and primped to pleasure the king.

At the end of this year, it was time to spend one night with the king. It was decision-making time for him. Who would win the contest? Each girl took her turn going "in to the king." When it was her turn, each girl was allowed to take with her "whatever she desired . . . from the harem (2:13)."

The main reason she won favor with Hegai was that God was sovereignly moving her into the place she needed to be.

> *Esther offered something more, perhaps something he had never seen in a woman. Could it have been the attributes that only a genuine faith in God can produce?*

They could choose clothing, jewelry, perfumes, ointments, or other objects. Most likely, it was whatever she thought would enhance her assets or increase her chance to make an impression on the king. Whatever her feelings were about the process, she knew that she would have a better life if she were to be chosen queen.

Once a girl spent her night with the king, she was taken to the second harem the next morning where she became one of the king's many mistresses. She was no longer a virgin and was therefore in a different category. She would never again return to the king unless he requested her by name. In fact, some of the concubines in the harem never saw the king again and spent the rest of their lives as lonely mistresses, with no chance of ever having a husband or a family (2 Sam 20:3).

Esther was one of the first to complete her 12-month treatment, so she was one of the first to go into the king. Hegai made sure of that. Her humility and teach-ability were demonstrated by the fact that she relied on Hegai's knowledge and experience (2:15). Obviously, a bond of trust had developed between them.

So, Esther went into the king. Wouldn't we love to know what was going on in her mind as she walked the palace halls to the king's chambers? Fear, dread, anticipation, surrender? Did she feel a sense of destiny? Did her faith give her strength to walk toward her duty?

The Scripture simply says, "The king loved Esther more than all the women (2:17)." We would love more details! Once again, we're left to use our imagination. It does go on to say that she "won grace and favor in his sight more than all the virgins (2:17)." This implies that she put some effort into winning him. The word "grace" implies that his affections were stirred beyond just sexual gratification. He had plenty of gratification at his disposal with his harem

Day 18

of concubines and virgins. Esther offered something more, perhaps something he had never seen in a woman. Could it have been the attributes that only a genuine faith in God can produce?

The differences between Vashti and Esther are apparent in spite of the limited information we have. Yes, they were both beautiful, but that is the one and only similarity. Vashti wore her beauty with arrogance and wielded her power with cruelty and superiority. Esther's beauty was enhanced by her grace, humility, and charm. What a stark contrast! The king must've been moved by the refreshing difference.

> Vashti wore her beauty with arrogance and wielded her power with cruelty and superiority. Esther's beauty was enhanced by her grace, humility, and charm. What a stark contrast!

After Esther's one night with the king, the contest was over. King Ahasuerus "set the royal crown on her head and made her queen instead of Vashti (2:17)." He didn't want to wait until he had sampled a few more women just in case—No! Esther impressed him to the point that he ended the search. Decision made. Crown assigned. Esther was made queen, and every mention of the previous queen was over.

Just like the ending of a great Disney movie, a wedding feast was thrown by the king to celebrate his new queen. He even called it "Esther's feast (2:18)." The king was so excited that he commemorated this exciting event with gifts of "royal generosity," and he even "granted a remission of taxes." God's personal queen was set in place and celebrated by a pagan empire.

Food for Thought When you think about Esther's journey to become the queen, does this whole process appall you? The one night "contest," the harem of virgins and concubines, the man who had all of these women at his disposal to meet the whims of his sexual desires. We cringe and mourn at the thought of any woman having to be a part of such a practice, especially our daughters. While most people are repulsed at the social injustice of keeping a harem full of women purely for the sexual gratification of a wealthy and powerful man, they refuse to see that pornography is essentially the same thing. Today, statistics reveal the mass acceptance of pornography by both men and women. According to an article on fightthenewdrug.org, 23 billion visits were made to a specific porn site in 2016 alone. That's 64 million per day. Yes, sexual lust is big business today!

Faith in Action Think about it. Any thought or activity that degrades a person and turns him or her into a sexual object to be used for one's own gratification, is a sin against that person and a sin against the Holy Spirit that resides in your body. Read 1 Corinthians 6:13-20 and Matthew 5:27-30. What does the Bible say about the sin of lust and pornography? If you are struggling with this sin, please seek help from your local church or a Christian counselor. Forgiveness and freedom are available to you through Christ.

What character traits do you see in Esther in chapter 2, from the time she was taken to the palace until the time she was crowned as queen? Write them down. Do you think that faith played any part in her attitude, thoughts, and behaviors? How so? The cultural environment she was thrust into was not conducive to a strong faith walk. However, she stood out among the others. She did not just blend in. Why do you think she was able to do this?

Prayer

Dear God, the temptations of this world are strong, and I can't fight them on my own. I need you. I need your truths to guide my thoughts and my steps. Remind me of my need for your grace, truth, and strength today and every day. Thank you for the example of Esther who stood out and stood strong in her pagan environment. With your help, I want to do the same.

Day 19

Esther 3:1–6

While the story of Esther hasn't been all butterflies and unicorns, in chapter 3 it takes an especially dark turn. Jeremiah 17:9 says, "The heart is *deceitful* above all things, and *desperately sick*; who can understand it? [emphasis mine]" The events in the next chapters will unquestionably illustrate this truth.

Mankind has struggled with feelings of prejudicial hatred toward others as far back as the first brothers, Cain and Abel (Gen 4). This kind of hatred, if left unchecked, can lead to dangerous intentions or even murder itself. We are all capable of this according to Jeremiah 17:9, and we need to be reminded of how dangerous prejudice can be.

We receive this lesson loud and clear through the character and actions of a man named Haman. He's the kind of villain that we all love to hate, because he had wealth and power, and he didn't mind using it to get ahead. He was self-serving and craved adulation—even if it had to be forced out of people. He wasn't just obnoxiously arrogant; his heart was filled with murderous, bigoted hate toward his enemies.

To understand Haman better, a little background history is in order. Haman was a descendant of the Amalekite king, Agag (1 Sam 15:1-33). But we have to go back even further to understand the beginning of the conflict between the Amalekites and the nation of Israel. Amalek was the grandson of Esau, and his people attacked Israel when they were leaving Egypt (Ex 17:8-16). Not only was

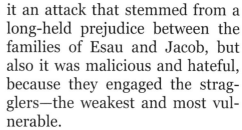

> Mankind has struggled with feelings of prejudicial hatred toward others as far back as the first brothers, Cain and Abel

it an attack that stemmed from a long-held prejudice between the families of Esau and Jacob, but also it was malicious and hateful, because they engaged the stragglers—the weakest and most vulnerable.

God cursed them for this unprovoked attack on the helpless and promised to "utterly blot out the memory of Amalek from under heaven (Ex 17:14)." God even reminded the Israelites of this directive in Deuteronomy 25:19, while outlining the details of the Law. God told them, "You shall not forget." Later, King Saul had a chance to fulfill this promise when God gave him a command through the prophet Samuel to destroy the Amalekites completely (1 Sam 15). Saul disobeyed the Lord's command and spared King Agag's life. As a result, Samuel carried out the Lord's directive and killed Agag himself. Because of this history of bad blood, a legacy of hate existed for 550 years. This long-held tribal feud was evident in Mordecai's refusal to bow to Haman, and by Haman's vicious desire to exterminate the Jews. Let's take a closer look at how Satan used their history in an attempt to thwart God's plan of redemption and destroy God's covenant promises.

Sometime between the seventh and twelfth year of King Ahasuerus' reign, Haman was elevated to a position that was "above all the officials who were with him (3:1)." It was a Persian custom that the people would bow to pay homage to those in positions of authority. So, all of the servants at the king's gate were commanded by the king to bow down to Haman when he passed.

All the officials bowed when Haman made his daily trip by the king's gate—except for Mordecai. There must have been so many officials that Haman failed to notice that Mordecai was standing. But Mordecai's fellow officials noticed, asked him the reason he disobeyed the king's

Day 19

command, and repeatedly warned him that he had better bow.

Mordecai must have tried to camouflage his actions, because he got away with it for a number of days. He even hid his reason for a time, until his co-workers browbeat it out of him. He had advised Esther not to tell anyone her nationality, yet he didn't heed his own advice. The reason he gave his peers for not bowing was that "he was a Jew (3:4)." The Expositor's Bible Commentary gives two potential explanations for the reason he wouldn't bow: 1) The religious reason—it would've been an act of idolatry; 2) The personal reason—he wouldn't be caught dead bowing to an Amalekite, the age-old enemy of his people (812).

While some try to spiritualize Mordecai's actions as being inspired by his faith, the evidence suggests his refusal was motivated by a pride and prejudice of his own. According to Herodotus, the act of bowing in the Persian court was a matter of etiquette rather than an act of worship (ESV Study Bible, 856). There are several instances in Scripture where people of faith bowed to a king in homage (Gen 23:7; 1 Sam 24:8; 1 Kg 1:16) as opposed to bowing to them in worship as a deity (Dan 3). Hence, we can deduce that Mordecai's refusal to bow to Haman was motivated by a personal prejudice. While he had warned Esther not to reveal her lineage, his personal pride and disdain for Haman would not allow him to keep it a secret himself.

Haman might never have known that Mordecai was standing had the other officials not ratted him out. They told Haman to "see whether Mordecai's words would stand (3:4)" or be tolerated. They probably asked Haman, "Are you going to let Mordecai get away with this? He says he's refusing to bow because he is a Jew." Haman's ugly hatred of the Jews was not a secret to these tattlers. It's impossible to hide hate as strong as Haman's, because inevitably, the one who

> We can deduce that Mordecai's refusal to bow to Haman was motivated by a personal prejudice.

30 Days to Ruth/Esther

This kind of hate is not satisfied with just hurting an individual. Most often, it seeks to destroy everything associated with the object of that hate.

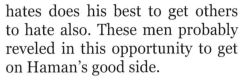

hates does his best to get others to hate also. These men probably reveled in this opportunity to get on Haman's good side.

Haman was "filled with fury (3:5)" at this news. His deep-seeded hatred and bigotry finally had a face. He didn't just want to destroy Mordecai alone, however; he schemed to "destroy all the Jews, the people of Mordecai (3:6)." His newly bestowed position gave him the ear of the king, and he set a plan in motion to utterly wipe out his enemy.

This is a cautionary example of how far-reaching a prejudice can be. This kind of hate is not satisfied with just hurting an individual. Most often, it seeks to destroy everything associated with the object of that hate. This was not to be a crime of passion—Haman didn't fly off the handle in a fit of rage because he lost control of his emotions. It would be a cruel, malicious, premeditated mass murder of an entire race of people. It is hard to fathom this kind of hatred! It should scare us into personal introspection.

Day 19

Food for Thought

Read these definitions of prejudice and hate. Think about how far back the prejudice illustrated in our story today can be traced. Pause to consider the depth of evil to which Haman was eager to go to satiate his prejudicial hatred. Since his childhood, he had watered this ideology, until it finally blossomed into an opportunity for action.

Prejudice – a preconceived judgment or opinion; an adverse opinion or leaning formed without just grounds or before sufficient knowledge; an irrational attitude of hostility; belief without basis or information.

Hate – intense hostility and aversion usually derived from fear, anger, or sense of injury.

Faith in Action

List some examples from history that portray this kind of prejudice and hate.

Ask yourself honestly if you possess any thoughts or feelings toward any individual or group of people that might be categorized as either prejudice or hate. Do not rush through this exercise of personal introspection. The repercussions are too dangerous. Consider that when you embrace any negative perception of others based on personal opinion or experience, insufficient information, or ethnic differences, prejudice is formed and a potential seed of hatred is planted. Be willing to ask God to reveal to you any seeds of prejudice and hate that reside in your mind or heart. Pray the words from Psalms 139:23-24 and listen to the Spirit's conviction.

Prayer

Father in heaven, I ask you to reveal any "grievous way in me." Shine the light of your truth into my heart and make me see any seed of prejudice and hate that exists. Don't allow me to make any excuses to cover up, rationalize, or defend any thought that is not pleasing to you. Help me to forgive and love as I have been forgiven and loved by you.

Day 20

Esther 3:7–15

Yesterday, Haman presented his devious, hate-filled scheme to the one person who could make his revenge fantasy a reality. In a scene reminiscent of a meeting of Nazi SS guards or a gathering of KKK members, a group of hate-filled men met to strategize the annihilation of a race of people they considered to be "different" than everyone else (3:8). They heartlessly rolled the dice to determine the day this mass genocide would take place.

These events happened during Nisan, the first month of the Jewish calendar—the very month that the Jews celebrated the Passover. How ironic that while the Jews met to celebrate their deliverance from the oppression of the Egyptians, Haman and his group met to plan their destruction.

The words that Haman used in his appeal to King Ahasuerus spoke to his character and the extent of his prejudicial hatred. As we look more carefully at his speech, we will recognize the similarity of the tactics and rationale used by those who seek to act upon their prejudice and hatred.

First, in verse 8, Haman emphasized that "their laws are different" from everyone else's. This was absolutely a true statement. No Jew would deny that fact. However, Haman used this truth as an indictment on them, as if it were a punishable thing to be different.

> *Most of our preconceived judgments are formed initially because of the way someone looks, thinks, or acts.*

Isn't being "different" the first rationale for prejudice? Most of our preconceived judgments are formed initially because of the way someone looks, thinks, or acts. Because it's in our nature to embrace and defend the way we look, think, or act, we naturally gravitate toward those who are just like us. While there is nothing inherently wrong with that, any time we exclude or devalue someone solely because they are "different" from us, we have succumbed to prejudice. We must be very intentional if we are to reverse this natural, sinful instinct.

Haman's next accusation was that "they do not keep the king's laws." This was in reference to Mordecai's refusal to bow. It did not apply to all the people, or even to Mordecai on the whole, so it was actually a false statement and a gross exaggeration. Haman took one incident and blew it out of proportion in hopes of fueling the king's anger to match his own. The implication was that these people would cause the king harm if he didn't take care of the problem. He sought to paint the Jewish people as unbending, rebellious, intolerant—people who didn't deserve to be tolerated themselves.

It has always been a very successful strategy to exaggerate and blow an incident out of proportion in order to get others to rally behind a prejudice. Most of the time a small piece of truth is used to create a plausible lie with the purpose of fueling fear and hatred. We see this played out in personal relationships, political agendas, and special interest groups. This should be a warning for each of us to eradicate this mentality from our personal lives.

The next statement was one of clever manipulation. Haman suggested that it was "not to the king's profit" to keep the Jews around. He knew that the royal treasury was running low from the king's unsuccessful war with Greece. He chose the perfect thing to mention to a power hungry and profit-seeking ruler. Then Haman brought out

Day 20

the big guns when he offered the king a bribe of 750,000 pounds of silver to be put directly into the hands of the king's bankers (3:9). We don't know if Haman was independently wealthy to be able to offer that sizable amount, or if he was counting on getting wealthy with the plunder of the Jews. Regardless, this final offer of his own personal wealth revealed how desperate he was in his quest to exact revenge in a most brutal and calculated way.

Haman must have said all of the right things to the king, because he was granted his wish. The king handed over his signet ring, which enabled Haman to act with the same authority as the king himself. King Ahasuerus also authorized Haman to use as much of the bribe money as he needed to carry out his plan. Finally, the king gave Haman "the people also (3:11)," as if they were his possessions to give away.

Things go terribly wrong any time profit trumps people. While Haman's main focus was revenge, the king's main focus was personal gain—to rid the land of a troublesome people, garner undying allegiance from one of his chief officials, and fill his treasuries, no matter the consequences. Sadly, this scenario is played out over and over again in our world today. The value of human life is at an all-time low, especially when a profit can be made. Unborn babies are killed in the name of convenience or profit making. Human beings are trafficked as property to be used for wanton pleasure while the traffickers gets rich. The elderly and those with special needs aren't given the care they deserve because of the cost to society. The marginalized in our communities are ignored because they have nothing to offer. These are not new problems in our society; they have been around for millennia.

The palace sprang into action following the royal decree. The king's scribes wrote page after page of announcements to get them into every known language

Most of the time a small piece of truth is used to create a plausible lie with the purpose of fueling fear and hatred.

127

> *Things go terribly wrong any time profit trumps people.*

in the realm. Once the letters were written, couriers mounted their horses and began their journeys to the far reaches of the kingdom. Every citizen needed to hear about the new law.

Look again at the words used in 3:13. The royal edict gave "instruction to destroy, to kill, and to annihilate all Jews, young and old, women and children . . . and to plunder their goods." These words were cold, heartless, and brutal, and they offered no loopholes. This was not the first time that Satan had used prejudice and hate in his attempt to derail God's covenant promises to the nation of Israel and his plan of redemption for all mankind. He always seems to find a human vessel filled with prejudice and hate to carry out his mission to thwart God's plans and nullify his promises (For further examples, study the evil Queen Athaliah in 2 Chr 22:10-12; Antiochus IV Epiphanes' attempt to wipe out the Jews and their culture; Herod's massacre of the innocents in Mt 2:16; Judas Iscariot's betrayal of Jesus in Lk 22:3-6; Adolf Hitler's agenda to exterminate Jews in WWII; and, the world's continued disdain for Israel.).

We close out this chapter with a chilling scene. Satan's plan was set in motion with Haman at the helm. Afterwards, Haman and the king "sat down to drink (3:15)." Haman reveled in celebratory satisfaction that his devious plan was coming together. The calloused king was unconcerned that he had signed the death warrants of a large population of his subjects and unaware that his own wife was among that number.

> *This was not the first time that Satan had used prejudice and hate in his attempt to derail God's covenant promises to the nation of Israel and his plan of redemption for all mankind.*

The city of Susa reeled with questions upon hearing this edict. Many of the citizens had personal or working relationships with their Jewish neighbors. This "confusion" offers a small glimmer of hope about the human race in an otherwise dark scene, for it implies that a majority were concerned about this dreadful law. Similarly, it proves that the majority did not share Haman's feelings of hatred toward the Jews.

> **Food for Thought**
>
> 550 years is a long time for a prejudice to stay alive! It is hard to fathom, and yet there are many stories from the pages of history, and from our present-day events, that tell of prejudices that exist and fester for centuries. Why do prejudices stay active for so long? Because, a prejudice is usually taught and then caught—exactly like our story in Esther. Prejudices are passed down through the generations, forced into the impressionable minds of children and reinforced through the actions of parents and cultures. How do we stop the seeds of prejudice and hatred from growing in our own hearts? How do we weed out any prejudices that have been fostered in our homes, communities, or society at large? Write down some of your thoughts here or discuss them with a fellow believer.

> **Faith in Action**
>
> The answers to the above questions (and all questions) are found in God's word! Read the following passages and write an answer, an encouragement, or a warning.
> - Proverbs 10:12
> - Proverbs 26:24-28
> - Matthew 5:21-26
> - Matthew 22:37-39
> - Romans 12:9-21
> - James 2:8-9
>
> What has God shown you about prejudice in the last two days? What are some things that you need to change in your attitudes, speech, and actions that demonstrate that you value every human as someone who has been created in the image of God?

Day 20

Prayer Father, I confess to you that I don't always love you with all my heart or love my neighbor as much as I should. Reveal to me that person or group of people that I am not valuing as your image bearers (i.e. a different ethnicity, people from another culture, someone who leads a different or sinful lifestyle, an irritating co-worker or classmate, a selfish family member, a frustrating spouse, etc.). Help me weed out any prejudices in my heart that have taken root. Show me a way that I can intentionally show love to someone that I do not value as I should. I also pray for all those in our world that are so full of hatred. May Christ-followers all over the globe continue to share that you are the only hope and the only answer to all of the evil in this world caused by prejudice and hate. Help me to start right where I live.

Esther 4

While "checkmate" seemed imminent in this cosmic chess game, God had other plans. The "Queen" was comfortable on her marbled square in her royal bubble, sipping tea and oblivious to the moves being made to take her out of the game. A deal had been struck for her life and the lives of her people. While her life had not been all that she had dreamed it would be as a young Jewish girl, she wasn't in fear for her life. She lived in a beautiful palace; she had servants who cared for her; and she was able to maintain a connection with her adoptive father. These were things for which she was thankful. Yet, her relationship with her husband, the King, was tenuous at best. After five years, she still never knew when or if his favor with her would run out or turn towards another. She never forgot that a Persian king lived according to momentary whims.

He must have requested her company fairly regularly until the events in chapter 4. But, it had been a whole month since she had spent time with him. Her thoughts were probably going haywire trying to understand the reasons for his absence, because in this scene, we find her a little on edge. But let's back up a little.

On the day that would change her life forever, her servants told her that Mordecai was outside the king's gate and something was terribly wrong. While they may not have known the reason, they knew Mordecai was important to her. They knew that she would want to know if something was wrong. They told her that Mordecai was

> Fear is an involuntary emotion brought on by a real or perceived threat outside of our control.

dressed in a hideous garment, had covered himself in ashes, and was walking around wailing at the top of his lungs. He looked like a madman, but he sounded really sad. In their royal bubble, evidently none of them had heard about the deadly edict.

We can only imagine what Esther must have thought at this news. She wanted to see him, so that she could find out what was happening. Mordecai was not allowed to come inside the gate in sackcloth and ashes, so Esther sent some proper clothes out to him; he refused them. Mordecai and Jews all over the kingdom were in great mourning because of the devastating announcement.

Esther sent Hathach, her most trusted eunuch, outside to talk to Mordecai. Hathach must have known their connection and ethnicity all along, because Mordecai trusted him with so much. Not only did Mordecai tell him everything, but he also gave him a copy of the edict so that Esther could look over it for herself. Mordecai asked Hathach to "show it . . . and explain it to her and *command* her" to do something about it—specifically to go to the king and beg for mercy on behalf of her people (4:8, emphasis mine).

Esther's response gives us a glimpse into the fears and insecurities in her heart. Let me paraphrase. "Everybody knows that no one can just waltz into the king's presence unannounced, even his wife. The law says that if you do, you could die. There is only one exception, and that's if the king holds out his scepter signaling that it's okay. I may not be the right one to go to him, because he hasn't wanted to see me in a month. If he's upset with me or done with me, he could have me killed on the spot. I can't help anyone if I'm dead! You might want to get someone else for this job."

Her response spoke loudest about the insecurity she felt in her relationship with the king. Even though she

Day 21

had been married to him for five years, her biggest emotion in regard to him was still fear. It was a big deal that she hadn't seen him in a month. Being replaced or deposed was always a viable possibility (Remember Vashti?). She definitely didn't speak with much confidence about going in to see him. Her first reaction screams that she was incredibly fearful about losing her own life—this was no small request from her father!

Mordecai's response in 4:13-14 sounded unsympathetic to her fears; even a little harsh. Again, I paraphrase. "You might think that because you are the queen that you'll be safe from this decree. You may think that if you sit silently by and don't cause a scene that you'll be able to hide that you are a Jew. But let me tell you that you will not be able to avoid this madman's mission. You and your father's family will die, and that includes me. However, I still believe that God will deliver the Jews somehow, some way, if not now then later, because he's made covenant promises to us. But think about this. Maybe, just maybe, God put you in this unique position so that he can use *you* at this crucial time."

This was the turning point for Esther. Something Mordecai said resonated with her, and her insecure fear turned into fledgling courage. Esther was not weak or wrong to be fearful for her life or her safety. In fact, fear is an involuntary emotion brought on by a real or perceived threat outside of our control. Therefore, fear, like any initial emotion, is not wrong. What one decides to do in response to those emotions determines a right or wrong course.

Which begs the question—What is the spark that ignites fear into a flame of courage? Is it merely survival instincts? Is it the pull of a noble mission or purpose? A large part of it has to be faith in something or someone greater than yourself, because fear is a very strong emotion to overcome.

> *Fear, like any initial emotion, is not wrong. What one decides to do in response to those emotions determines a right or wrong course.*

Courage is an act of the will in response to fear and in spite of fear.

The Merriam-Webster definition of courage is "the mental or moral strength to venture, persevere, and withstand danger, fear, or difficulty." So, courage is an act of the will in response to fear and in spite of fear. In Esther's case, 4:15 records the exact moment in time that she made the decision that her fear would not hold her back from her God-ordained destiny. She could have refused to act. She could have retreated back into her comfort zone, what she knew, her "normal." She could have decided to try to continue to hide who she was—it had worked so far. But she didn't do any of those things. She decided to venture into the danger and to withstand any difficulty that could result.

However, she did an extremely wise thing; she didn't rush headlong into a solution. She asked for help and gave herself some time. She told Mordecai to find every Jew he could find and ask them to fast for three days. While prayer is not mentioned here, it is heavily implied. She committed herself and her closest attendants to do the same. In conclusion, she boldly declared, "*Then* I will go to the king, though it is against the law, and if I perish, I perish (4:16, emphasis mine)."

This statement demonstrated her resolve to do the right thing. She mentioned the life-threatening danger again when she said that it was against the law. This indicated that her fear was still very real. Yet, she proclaimed that she was willing to die for this cause, and she believed that her life was in God's hands.

We can proceed with courage because our confidence and trust is in God who always knows best and fulfills his purposes.

Esther offered a wise example of what we should do when faced with important decisions that are laced with fear. We should pray and ask for others to pray

Day 21

with us. We should engage in a focused time of seeking God's wisdom and help. James 1:5-8 promises us that if we need wisdom then we should "ask God . . . and it will be given." Then, we can proceed with courage because our confidence and trust is in God who always knows best and fulfills his purposes.

Food for Thought

Do you have any fears that are weighing you down today? What is the circumstance in your life that causes you to worry or dread every time you think about it? Do you feel paralyzed, either not knowing what to do or scared to do what you should? Are you hiding or running from something? Is your fear causing you to pretend that all is well so that others will think that things are fine? What will you do with that fear? Contemplate the following quotes about courage:

"Courage is not the absence of fear, but rather the judgment that something else is more important than fear." Ambrose Redmoon

"Courage is not living without fear. Courage is being scared to death and doing the right thing anyway." Chae Richardson

"I learned that courage was not the absence of fear, but the triumph over it." Nelson Mandela

"Courage is resistance to fear, mastery of fear... not absence of fear." Mark Twain

While these quotes are inspiring and accurate, they do not identify the source of the required mental or moral strength that gives us courage. Let me submit that all of us are born with the capacity for courage, because we are created in the image of God. Whether we identify him as the source or not depends on whether we know him personally. Those who are not children of God will identify this source as "something" greater than themselves. For the child of God, it is a faith and trust in him who is greater and bigger than any circumstance we may face. We can do this because we can acknowledge that he is in control of everything. Read the above quotes again and identify and give glory to God who is the source of courage for the child of God.

Do your fears affect your faith in God or does your faith in God determine how your fears will affect you?

Day 21

Faith in Action

Read the following verses and answer the questions.

- Deuteronomy 31:6, 8 – Why could the people be strong and courageous instead of being fearful and dismayed?

- Joshua 1:6-9 – What was the responsibility that God required of Joshua to go along with his promises of strength, courage, and presence?

- Psalm 27:14; 31:24 – What action is required for strength and courage?

- Philippians 1:20-21 – What was the purpose for which Paul desired full courage?

- 2 Timothy 1:7 – How does this verse encourage you to triumph over fear?

Prayer

Thank you, Father, for the courageous example of Esther, who in spite of her fears entrusted herself to you and resolved to do the right thing no matter the danger. I surrender my fears to you. Give me courage! I don't want my fears to hold me back from fulfilling your purpose for Christ to be honored with my life. Thank you for your promised presence. I look to you and wait for you to give me strength and courage.

Day 22

Esther 5

Never had makeup been more carefully applied, hair been more meticulously coiffed, or an outfit given such detailed attention. Esther wanted to be resplendent as she stood before the king. She wanted his first glance to be a vivid reminder of who she was to him and why he had chosen her to be his queen. It's an understatement to say that Esther's goal was to dress for success—she needed the king to be eating out of her hand before the day was over.

We can only imagine how nervous Esther must have been as she walked down the corridor toward the throne room. The fear she battled as she stood in his line of sight and waited for his response was tangible. He had cruelly banished one queen for not coming to him when summoned. She knew full well that he could punish her for coming to him without being invited.

It's hard for us to understand how truly dangerous this was. We are accustomed to waltzing into just about anywhere because we have freedom and rights. While there are certain places and people that we cannot access, we aren't afraid that they might have us killed if we wander into their presence. So, Esther's situation is a foreign concept to us. Literally, her life hung in the balance as she stood in the court and waited.

Did King Ahasuerus' heart skip a beat? Did he catch his breath at the sight of her? Was his curiosity stirred? Whatever the reason, he held out the golden scepter that signaled his approval for Esther to approach him. In re-

> *The elaborate plan that Esther implemented was a study in wise strategies for business dealings and healthy relationships: understanding your audience, being prepared, patient implementation, not allowing your emotions to lead the way, doing your best, and working toward excellence.*

spect for the royal customs of the day, Esther came near enough to touch the tip of the scepter. The king knew that Esther took a risk to try to see him; it was highly unusual. Immediately, he asked her what she wanted. He knew that she must want something pretty badly to come to him without being called. The statement that he made in 5:3 is not to be taken literally; it was a grand gesture and implied that he would grant her wish if at all possible.

Esther responded with a shrewd request. "I've prepared a small feast for you, my husband, and would like for you to bring Haman along and come eat with me." As every smart woman knows, there is a proper time and way to make requests. It is wise to avoid important conversations when someone is tired or "hangry" (defined as "bad-tempered or irritable as a result of hunger"). The queen wanted the king satisfied from a delicious meal and relaxed and happy from the wine. Most likely, she asked Haman to tag along because she wanted him overconfident and cocky. She wanted him to be totally blindsided when she explained exactly how his devious plan had put her in danger.

Every aspect of the meal was part of a grand design that Esther created for optimum results. The finest tableware, the king's favorite dishes, the best wine, and the sparkling dinner conversation were all a part of her strategy. Esther displayed incredible patience, which probably piqued the king's curiosity even more. Finally, he asked again, "What is your wish?"

> *A heart full of hate can never stay happy, because hate always pushes out any positive emotion.*

Day 22

She held his attention a while longer as she continued the role of a woman of mystery; she asked them both to a second feast the next day where she promised to reveal her request.

The elaborate plan that Esther implemented was a study in wise strategies for business dealings and healthy relationships: understanding your audience, being prepared, patient implementation, not allowing your emotions to lead the way, doing your best, and working toward excellence. This kind of wisdom can be ours when we ask God for it—just like Esther did.

The second invitation swelled Haman's big head even more, and he felt on top of the world. But a heart full of hate can never stay happy, because hate always pushes out any positive emotion. As Haman walked past the king's gate, Mordecai's continual refusal to bow filled him with rage. Even the favorable attention of the king and queen could not abate his fury. He not only wanted Mordecai on his face in front of him but trembling in fear of the power he held over him.

With true egotistical narcissism, Haman called together his wife and friends to recount for them all the reasons he was so awesome. They had heard this speech ad nauseam. They were probably all checked out of this brag fest when Haman finally said, "And today, I had lunch with the king and queen. Queen Esther even invited me to eat with them again tomorrow." Between the "oo's" and "ah's," they noticed that Haman was pouting, not smiling. He continued, "But none of this means anything to me as long as that Jew, Mordecai, refuses to bow down to me. He should be shaking in his boots when I walk by (5:13, paraphrase mine)."

While it seemed that Haman held Mordecai's life in his hands, the one who holds all things in his hands had other plans.

While he calculated the days until the edict erased Mordecai from his life, his vicious wife and friends presented a more expedient solution. They proposed that he kill Mordecai without delay. With all the power and favor of the new position at his disposal, they urged him to ask the king to have Mordecai hanged. Full of confidence and vengeful delight, he used his power and resources to custom-build the biggest, highest gallows for his arch nemesis. While it seemed that Haman held Mordecai's life in his hands, the one who holds all things in his hands had other plans.

Day 22

> **Food for Thought**

A study in the sovereignty of God could lead you to believe that all you need do is sit back, relax, and let God do his thing. However, the seemingly incongruous truths of God's sovereignty and man's responsibility are equally illustrated in the pages of Scripture. The Books of Ruth and Esther illustrate both these truths beautifully. Esther 5 is all about Esther being intricately involved in God working out the deliverance of his people. She was extremely active in the process: fasting, praying, seeking God's face, strategically planning, using her wits, wisdom, beauty, and charm.

Look back at Day 9 to be reminded of another example of God using the actions and plans of people to carry out his sovereign plan. Naomi was active in her strategic planning with Ruth and Boaz.

What blessings are you missing out on because you refuse to act in accordance with God's sovereign plans in a particular situation? Have you asked God for wisdom and direction in what you can be doing or how he wants to use you to carry out his plans? Don't get me wrong. This does not give us license to rush ahead in our own wisdom and strength to "fix" problems or manipulate solutions. But neither does it mean that we should cower in our comfort zones, unwilling to move past our fears, insecurities, and inabilities. God has always used his children to carry out his plans and purposes, because he wants us to receive the blessings and benefits of him working through us. Don't let your lack of courage keep you from recognizing where God is at work and joining him there.

Faith in Action

Let's think some more about Esther approaching the king's throne, hoping to gain access to him and receive his favor. This was the case for all who lived in times where kings ruled kingdoms. Gaining access to the king was difficult and required a stringent protocol. You couldn't just show up any time you wanted to ask the king something, even if you were his wife.

Many times, we live as though we cannot gain access to our king, Jesus Christ. We run to anyone but him when we are faced with fears and difficulties. We exhaust every other solution we can think of before asking the one with all the answers. Does fear keep us from going to God first with our problems? Does pride or self-sufficiency? Or, is it that we really don't believe that he hears us and stands ready to listen and help us?

Queen Esther feared for her safety when going before the king's throne. In contrast, Hebrews 4:16 says "Let us then with confidence draw near to the throne of grace, that we may receive mercy and find grace to help in time of need." The word "confidence" means with boldness and courage. How wonderful that in the throne room of King Jesus we don't face fear or judgment but a "throne of grace." When we are "in time of need"—needing help, mercy and grace—our first stop should be on our knees before the throne of grace.

Read the Scriptures below and write how these truths encourage you.

- Romans 5:2 -

- Ephesians 2:18 -

- Ephesians 3:12 -

- James 4:8 –

Day 22

Prayer

Dear Jesus, I approach your throne today acknowledging that you are my King. I bow in surrender to you and your will. I lay my needs before you and ask for mercy, grace, and help. I come with boldness and confidence, because I trust you to keep your promises to help me. I also ask for spiritual eyes to see where you are working and for wisdom and guidance for how you want me to join you. Give me courage to ask for wisdom and then act in obedience!

Day 23

Esther 6

After we could read and write words in Elementary School, we began to learn to be creative. Even before we could spell decently, we were encouraged to use our imagination to create stories. Remember that the five essential elements of a story are characters, setting, plot, conflict, and resolution. Every novel we've read since then contains these elements.

While the contents of the Book of Esther are so much more than a mere "story," and undeniably a vital part of the Jews' history, we see all of the elements in this story. By chapter 6, we know the characters and the setting pretty well. An understanding of the redemptive metanarrative of Scripture informs us of the plot—the preservation of the promised seed through the nation of Israel (specifically through the Davidic line as outlined in the Book of Ruth). This is important so that God's plan of redemption for all people will be carried out through the life, death, and resurrection of the promised Messiah, Jesus Christ. In the shadow of the gallows that Haman built for his enemy Mordecai, we see the conflict in all of its gruesome detail. The climax of the story is in chapter 7, and the resolution is covered in the last three chapters of the book. Now, for chapter 6.

While Haman lay in his bed satisfied with his plan to exact revenge on his enemy, King Ahasuerus tossed and turned in his royal bed until he could stand it no longer. The king called for the history books to be read to him.

> *Our innate sense of justice is delighted as we read Haman detail the way he desired to be honored.*

Maybe he wanted something that would put him to sleep, or maybe he wanted his ego stroked with reminders of his exploits. Whatever the reason, when the royal readers opened the chronicles, the book fell open to the story of Mordecai's discovery of an assassination plot on the king's life (2:19-23).

Herodotus recounted in his ancient histories that it was a "point of honor" for Persian kings to reward those who did them favors (EBC, 822). Usually the reward came quickly and profoundly. As a result, when the account didn't end with a record of a reward given to Mordecai for his act of loyalty, the king jumped to remedy this oversight. Mordecai's "due season" was about to happen (See Day 17; Gal 6:9).

Meanwhile, Haman set his alarm clock for the earliest possible time to head to the palace so that he would be first on the king's docket to make his murderous request. With a pep in his step, he arrived in the courtyard before anyone else was even up. Imagine his delight when one of the king's attendants came to get him and told him that the king wanted to see him right away. His head was so big at this point that he probably had a hard time getting through the doorway. Then, he was asked an amazing question by the king: "Tell me what I should do for the person I wish to honor." Well, Haman could hardly contain himself. His arrogance reached new heights as he customized a plan to receive the grandest honors he could imagine for himself. He salivated at the prospect of being treated like royalty—dressed in one of the king's own robes, seated on top of the king's own thoroughbred stallion, wearing one of the king's crowns, while a royal official shouted to all the people that the king delighted to honor him. "Why, this is almost like being the king myself," he probably thought.

Honestly, we begin to revel at this turn of events, as we begin to see the villain Haman get what he deserves. Our innate sense of justice is delighted as we read Haman

Day 23

detail the way he desired to be honored. Then came the most unexpected words from the king; words that must have filled Haman's heart with rage and dread: "Do so to Mordecai the Jew (6:10)." Don't you just want to stand up and cheer? Maybe we shouldn't rejoice in the utter humiliation of Haman, but it's hard not to feel grateful that justice was served. Not only was Haman deprived of the royal treatment he so craved, but he was the one who had to bestow it on the man he hated the most.

> Maybe we shouldn't rejoice in the utter humiliation of Haman, but it's hard not to feel grateful that justice was served.

When his duty was done, he practically ran from the scene "mourning and with his head covered (6:12)." His own plans for Mordecai and the Jews had sent them into mourning just a few short days ago. Here, the king's plans for Mordecai sent him into mourning—this was divine irony. Even his wife and friends seemed to see the handwriting on the wall and prophesied defeat (6:13).

We are left to wonder how Mordecai felt, thought, or responded to this show of honor from the king that was carried out by Haman. Verse 12 simply says that Mordecai went back to his job as soon as the fanfare was over. While Haman was humiliated, it appeared that Mordecai showed humility. He simply went back to doing what he had always been doing. The show of honor did not change the fact that his people were still in danger, and that is what mattered the most to him. Mordecai's response of faithfulness and humility is a beautiful contrast to Haman's arrogance and hate. Indeed, the tide was turning!

> While Haman was humiliated, it appeared that Mordecai showed humility.

This chapter is filled with wonderful, "divine coincidences." As in the Book of Ruth (2:3; Day 6), what seem to be coincidences are actually evidences of God's providence at work. First, insomnia just happened to hit the king "that night (6:1)." Second, the story of Mordecai saving the king "was found" and read to the king, even though five years of history had passed (6:2). Third, "Haman had just entered" the court when the king was looking for somebody to carry out his plan to honor Mordecai (6:4). All of this is proof that the divine "grandmaster" was moving the chess pieces into position for "checkmate." More on that, tomorrow.

> *Mordecai's response of faithfulness and humility is a beautiful contrast to Haman's arrogance and hate.*

Day 23

Food for Thought

While Esther was in the midst of a clever plan to rescue her people, God was at work from his end. There is an important lesson in this for us today. Sometimes we may feel like things are not moving in the right direction or fast enough. We may be praying, seeking God's face, and asking for wisdom, but we're not seeing any benefits from our obedience. Our faith is faltering, because we cannot see him working, and we are weary and losing heart. Never forget that when we act in obedience to God's direction we are never acting alone. While God desires to use us as human instruments in his plans and purposes, he is still the one working and in complete control. Faith in this truth should banish fear from our hearts and energize us with courage. Remember that he has gone before us making preparations that we cannot even see (Eph 3:20-21). His ways and timing are so different than ours (Is 55:8-9). His Spirit is within us empowering us to accomplish his will and filling us with his presence for courage, wisdom, and whatever ability we need for a given situation (Eph 3:16; Phil 2:13).

Faith in Action

Write down on index cards or post-it notes the three important truths highlighted in today's reading. Don't forget to look up the Scriptures. Read and recite these truths several times throughout the day. Apply them to your life and let them transform your thinking and living today.

1. God's divine plans cannot be thwarted by anyone or anything. Trust! (Job 42:2; Ps 33:10-12; Pr 19:21)

2. God IS at work and his ways and timing are perfect. Be obedient and patient! (2 Sam 22:31; Ps 86:8-12; Is 40:31; Rom 8:28; Phil 1:6)

3. Beware the sin of pride! It brings devastating consequences. (Ps 31:23; Pr 11:2; 16:18; 29:23)

Prayer

Father, today I declare that I will trust you because you are in control. Nothing can hinder your plans and purposes—not even me. I acknowledge that you are at work and that your ways and timing are perfect. I will believe that with my whole heart even if I can't see what you are doing right now. I'll just keep seeking you, obeying you, and waiting for you to fulfill your purposes in my life and in the lives of those I love. Reveal to me any pride in my heart that is keeping me from all the good that you have for me.

Day 24

Esther 7

While Haman was receiving a bad prophecy from his wife and friends, the king's eunuchs arrived at his house and whisked him away to the second feast prepared by Esther for the king and him. If Haman did feel any comfort or assurance from sitting down with the royal couple, it was to be short-lived. The king lost no time in making a third request to hear Esther's wish (7:2). Curiosity has a way of keeping one's attention, right? Esther knew this, and after his third request, she knew that she had the king's full attention.

This was it! Now was the time for the big reveal! Esther could hide behind her crown no longer, her heritage shrouded in mystery and obscurity. This was her "for such a time as this" moment. And with God's help, Esther handled it with dignity, clarity, and ingenuity.

Holding the king's undivided attention, she answered, "If you have any love and favor in your heart for me at all, I ask you to save my life and the lives of my people (7:3, paraphrase mine)." Anticipating the giant question mark the king would have at this statement, she proceeded. "For, you see, the lives of my people and I have been sold to be destroyed, to be killed, and to be annihilated (3:13)." Queen Esther cleverly used the exact words from the edict, perhaps as an attempt to jog the king's memory of what this was about.

She could have been accusatory and said, "I can't believe you took a bribe in exchange for the lives of me and

> *Esther could hide behind her crown no longer, her heritage shrouded in mystery and obscurity. This was her "for such a time as this" moment.*

my people." But she was smart and knew that making accusatory statements to someone (especially one's king or spouse) puts him on the defensive and usually doesn't accomplish much good.

The statement she made next in verse 4 is obscure in the Hebrew, and its interpretation is routinely discussed by theologians. The most popular interpretation is that she understood the king's personality and values, and she appealed to his self-interest and desire for monetary profit. In essence she said, "If only we had been sold into slavery, I would not have even troubled you with a request. To eliminate us will be a great financial loss to you compared to what you could have made if our enemy had simply sold us into slavery." In a nice way, she implied that the king had been duped. She knew that financial profit was important to the king; she hoped that her life was too.

We have to assume that King Ahasuerus was unaware that the edict he allowed Haman to craft was specifically for the Jewish people. He definitely had no idea at that moment that Queen Esther was a Jew herself. Look back at 3:8 and notice that the description Haman used was "a certain people." He never specifically identified those "certain people" as the Jews. After all, the king didn't hesitate to honor Mordecai, and he had publicly declared his Jewish heritage. However, the king's cavalier attitude in agreeing to the edict speaks to his lack of value for human life. In fact, his hasty agreement highlighted his self-serving motivations—power, profit, and catering to others who were the same. It's hard for us to accept a king being so self-serving and indifferent about human life, but it's just as common today as it was back then.

> *She knew that financial profit was important to the king; she hoped that her life was too.*

Day 24

The king, who had obviously not connected the dots, was appalled that anyone had "dared" to devise a plan that would kill his queen. In fact, when Queen Esther pointed her finger at Haman and called him a "foe and enemy," the king was so angry that he had to leave the room to compose himself and collect his thoughts. His mind reeled with what this meant. His wife's life was in danger; his most trusted official had planned it; when did this happen? Wait, the edict... That meant that the beautiful woman that he had chosen for his queen was one of the people that he had ordered to be annihilated. Had Haman known when he talked him into this edict? What was Haman up to? Should I have trusted him?

So many emotions must have been going through the king's mind—fear for his wife; anger at the betrayal of Haman; and maybe, regret for his part in it. We don't know how long he took in the palace garden, but plenty went on while he was out of the room.

Once the king stormed out of the room, the queen was left with Haman, who was in all out panic mode. Haman wasn't dumb—he knew that he was in mortal danger. He knew that Esther was talking about his edict; he just didn't know that she was one of the people he hated so thoroughly. His thoughts raced as he scrambled to find a way out of his predicament. "How did this woman from that despicable race ever become queen? It's obvious that the king believed her and was furious. My only hope is mercy!"

In desperation, and without consideration for proper appearances, Haman fell on Queen Esther's couch to beg for his life. In another moment of providential, "perfect timing," the king re-entered the room at the moment when Haman inappropriately invaded Esther's personal space. With the king's negative mindset, things went from bad to worse. He

The king ordered that he be hung on the very gallows at his house that he had built for Mordecai. The cosmic gavel fell as final, and poetic, justice was served.

knew that Haman despised all Jews, so it wasn't a leap to believe that Haman was assaulting the queen in the palace, even with the king in the next room.

As soon as King Ahasuerus accused Haman of assault against the queen, the same attendants that brought Haman to the feast placed a hood over his head and hurried him out to his execution. The king ordered that he be hung on the very gallows at his house that he had built for Mordecai. The cosmic gavel fell as final, and poetic, justice was served.

Day 24

Food for Thought

Proverbs 26:27 says, "Whoever digs a pit will fall into it, and a stone will come back on him who starts it rolling." (See also Ps 7:15 and Eccl 10:8) What happened to Haman was an exact fulfillment of that principle. This is a cautionary example for all of us. When we throw a "stone" of gossip, unkindness, or disdain, remember these words from Scripture. If we devise plans (i.e. "dig a pit") to trap someone, even if we think they deserve it, get ready for a personal stumble. The biblical answer to being wronged is not judgment but mercy (James 2:13). God's way for us to treat all people is with grace and mercy (Read Lk 6:31-38; Mt 7:1-2).

Queen Esther courageously brought to light the evil that had been planned for her people. We have established that she carried out this plan with wisdom, after careful consideration, fasting, and prayer. Did you notice what was missing from her response to the king? She could have requested that Haman be punished with the severest punishment, but she didn't. She could've used her "up to half of the kingdom" offer from the king to ensure that Haman got what he deserved, but she didn't. She may have had in mind the words of God given to Moses in Deuteronomy 32:35-36, "Vengeance is mine, and recompense. . . . For the LORD will vindicate his people and have compassion on his servants." She left punishment specifics to the king, and ultimately, to the Lord (Rom 12:19; Heb 10:30).

Faith in Action

While Esther certainly had a right to rejoice that Haman was getting what he deserved, we don't see her doing that. It's hard not to rejoice when someone's evil deeds are uncovered and punished, but Scripture warns us against doing so. Read Proverbs 24:17-20. Write down what a proper response should be to God's justice. What about when it seems that evil is prevailing? Think about the difference between *rejoicing that the effects of evil are stopped and being glad that an evil person will suffer.*

Do you ever hear yourself wish that something bad would happen to someone who has wronged you? Confess that sin and use God's word to help you find a better way to think and pray about that person and the situation.

Prayer

Father of mercy and grace, please give me grace and mercy as I deal with people, especially the ones who have wronged me. Help me to trust you and leave vengeance in your hands, knowing that you are the God of justice and will judge people rightly. Forgive me for harboring any ill will against anyone. Give me the right thoughts and attitudes towards others today.

Day 25

Esther 8

Who doesn't love a good rescue story? The kind that comes complete with a white knight, a superhero, or someone willing to risk his or her life for the sake of another? Many of the movies we love have this story line. We hold our breath as we watch someone in danger, fearing for her life, fighting with everything she has. Just when all hope seems lost, the hero bursts onto the scene and rescues her. Finally, we exhale and wait for our hearts to resume a normal rhythm. And, we applaud the hero and breathe a sigh of relief for the one who was rescued.

The truth is that every one of us needs to be rescued. We all need a hero at different points in our lives. We need a deliverer because we cannot deliver ourselves. It may be a task that we find impossible to accomplish on our own. It may be a financial disaster over which we have no control. It may be a sickness or disease that we are powerless to cure. We may even need rescuing from someone who wishes to do us harm. Ultimately, we all need to be rescued from our own sinfulness, that keeps us captive to our selfish desires and emotions. For this, we need a superhero—or a supreme-hero.

Stories of divine, heroic deliverance are scattered through the Old Testament. God delivered the children of Israel from Egyptian bondage through Moses. On many occasions, God delivered the Jews from enemy oppression through various judges. Through the warrior-king David, God delivered his people from all their enemies. Then,

> *The truth is that every one of us needs to be rescued.*

they experienced a period of peace under Solomon, unlike anything they had before or since. Here, we see the divine deliverance of Esther and her people. All of these stories of deliverance foreshadow the coming of the supreme hero and deliverer, Jesus Christ, who fulfilled God's ultimate purpose to rescue people from the curse of Satan, sin, death, and hell. That is a reason to rejoice and worship!

Now, back to our story. Haman was dead and the "wrath of the king abated (7:10)," but deliverance for the Jews was not secured. In chapter 8, King Ahasuerus and Queen Esther had their heads together, discussing the problem. Persian custom dictated that the property of criminals be confiscated by the king. So, the first thing that Ahasuerus did was give all of Haman's property to Queen Esther. We can imagine that he was trying to make up for Esther's pain the only way he knew how—by giving her something profitable. Esther explained to the king exactly who she was and how she was connected with the other Jew that he knew, Mordecai. As all the details came into focus for the king, he invited Mordecai into his presence.

What the king did next was pivotal. He gave Mordecai his signet ring, previously held by Haman, which elevated Mordecai to prime minister and empowered him to act in the king's name. Esther then gave her newly acquired property to her adopted father. Mordecai had position, property, and power, given to him by his king, but divinely arranged by the sovereign God of the universe.

At that point, Esther was overwhelmed in her desperation. She could not hold it together any longer. While Haman had been defeated and her father had been rewarded, her people were still under a death sentence. She lost all reserve, broke down, fell at her husband's feet, and begged him to do something to stop this evil plan. The king had never seen his queen so distraught. Not knowing what else to do, he held out his scepter again and hoped that Es-

Day 25

ther would regain composure (few men really know what to do with a sobbing woman).

Once again, Esther demonstrated great courage as she pulled herself together enough to carefully articulate her desire. While she was extremely emotional, she did not let her emotions override her intellect. Wisely, she appealed to the king's favor of her. She was careful to place the blame for the wicked plot on Haman, not the king. She asked that the king write something that would overrule or "revoke" the previous edict.

The king reminded his wife that he had done what he could—destroyed her people's enemy and empowered her father to act. Yet, he acknowledged that he was powerless to revoke the edict. He suggested that she write another edict as she pleased. With that statement, the king declared it out of his hands. He left the solution in the hands of his queen and his new prime minister.

The scene in verses 9 through 14 is almost identical to the scene in 3:12-15. Scribes, letters, signet rings, couriers, fast horses, provinces, even the wording of the second edict is a paraphrase of the first edict. The second edict was written to neutralize the first one, however. Yes, everyone that wanted to participate in the attempt to "destroy, to kill, and to annihilate all Jews . . . and to plunder their goods (3:13)" were still empowered to do so. However, the second edict gave the Jews permission to "destroy, to kill, and to annihilate any . . . people . . . that might attack them . . . and to plunder their goods (v. 11)." In other words, the Jews were given the right to defend themselves to the degree that they were attacked.

For the second time in a matter of days, Mordecai was honored in Susa in a public way. No one argued against Mordecai's exalted position when they saw him in the royal robes of blue and white, fine linen, and purple. The second time he wore a great golden crown was not just to be honored but to

All of these stories of deliverance foreshadow the coming of the supreme hero and deliverer, Jesus Christ.

163

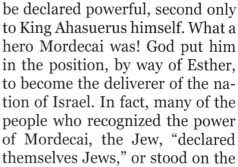

> The Jews were given the right to defend themselves to the degree that they were attacked.

be declared powerful, second only to King Ahasuerus himself. What a hero Mordecai was! God put him in the position, by way of Esther, to become the deliverer of the nation of Israel. In fact, many of the people who recognized the power of Mordecai, the Jew, "declared themselves Jews," or stood on the side of the Jews, because they feared the power that the king's favor had granted them.

Verses 15 through 17 describe a scene of relief and rejoicing among the Jewish residents of Susa and some Persian residents as well. Perhaps the Persian residents who "shouted and rejoiced" were the same ones who were "thrown into confusion (3:15)" over the first edict. The Jews acted as anyone who has been rescued from certain death would act—with "light and gladness and joy and honor (v. 16)."

Two months and ten days of heart-breaking sadness and bone-chilling fear had gone by since the first edict. Then came the news of deliverance. However, there was still 8 months and 20 days until the two, joint edicts took effect. Now, however, the Jews knew that they would be able to protect themselves when the fateful day arrived. While it isn't stated, we can be sure that their celebration included praise and worship of their great God, who had changed the unchangeable and rescued his people.

Day 25

Food for Thought

Esther knew that a king's edict was unchangeable and could not be revoked. So why did she ask him to revoke it? She didn't just want to give up on an impossible problem, so she asked, "Is there a way?" Perhaps this is evidence of the fact that she had faith that God would make a way to rescue his people—she just didn't know how he would. Do you agree?

Jesus told us to "Ask . . . seek . . . knock." Read Matthew 7:7-11. Sometimes when we ask, it reveals that we believe that God can do what we're asking, we just don't yet know how he will. It reveals that we are aware of our need. Our asking is evidence that we are going to the right source for rescue, solutions, and help. However, in our asking we should not demand that God do it our way, but in surrender, trust that he knows what's best and will accomplish his will.

What do you need to ask God? Acknowledge your desperate need of rescue. Seek his wisdom, his guidance, and his will. Knock on those doors of impossibility and wait to see how God will accomplish his purposes.

Faith in Action

How many things can you name that are unchangeable or seem unchangeable? Make a list. How many things can you list that are always changing? Hopefully you immediately listed God as unchangeable. And since we've been studying the Book of Esther, I'm sure you also identified a Persian king's edict as unchangeable. What current circumstance of your life seems unchangeable?

What about unsolvable problems? Are there any of those in your life right now? Do you need deliverance from a seemingly impossible situation in your life? Esther and her people were faced with the unsolvable *problem of an unchangeable edict. Apart from God, there was no escape route and no deliverer in sight—their annihilation had been placed on the calendar. But as we've already seen, the unchangeable God is in the business of solving the unsolvable and changing the unchangeable. He is the ultimate hero and divine deliverer!*

Read the following verses and write how each one encourages you.
- *Genesis 18:9-14 -*

- *Jeremiah 32:17, 27 -*

- *Luke 18:27 -*

Prayer

God, I praise you that you are unchangeable. In this world of constant change, I can anchor my soul in who you are and will always be. I can trust that through every circumstance, no matter how difficult or impossible it may seem, I can trust that you are working and fulfilling your divine purposes in my life and in the world. I thank you that you are my powerful deliverer, my merciful rescuer, and my supreme-hero!

Day 26

Esther 9–10

The day arrived—the 13th day of the 12th month, in the year 473 BC. For almost nine months, both sides had prepared to take their stand. On one side, the Jew-haters strategized to kill as many Jews as they could and take as much plunder as they could. On the other side, the Jews prepared to defend themselves against any and all attackers. God's deliverance of his people did not come as it had in Egypt, when he led them out and through the Red Sea and destroyed their enemies with a wave of Moses' arm. This time deliverance came in the form of permission to fight back and defend themselves against those who hated them and wanted to destroy them.

Up until chapter 9, only Haman's hatred of the Jews had been emphasized in the book. But here, we find that he was not the only one who hated them. Apparently, there was a vicious, widespread prejudice against the Jews. The numbers provide the evidence. 810 men in Susa, who wanted to kill their Jewish neighbors, were killed themselves (500 the first day, 300 the second day, and Haman's 10 sons). 75,000 people who acted on their hate-filled prejudice were struck down by the Jews in all of the other provinces. There are no casualties listed for the Jews, because they had providential protection.

There are a few interesting tidbits for us to note among the details of this day of fighting. First, it says that fear of the Jews had fallen on all the people (9:3). During the eight months after Mordecai became prime minis-

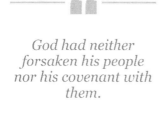

> *God had neither forsaken his people nor his covenant with them.*

ter, he had become famous and very powerful (9:4). Everyone in the Persian empire knew that the prime minister was a Jew, and that the queen herself was a Jew. This caused many to rethink their opinions and prejudices. The higher officials in all of the provinces also took note of the king's favor toward Mordecai, and in true political fashion, switched their votes in favor of the Jews and began to help them (9:3).

Second, it's important to note that while the Jews were given permission to plunder those who attacked them, they chose not to do it. In every instance where statistics were given, it added that the Jews "laid no hand on the plunder (9:10, 15, 16)." This fact proved that the Jews were careful to stay focused on the main objective—the preservation of their race. They wanted no profit from this horrendous event. They were not happy that they were given permission to kill their enemies; they were glad because they were given the chance to defend their lives, families, and possessions.

Third, isn't it interesting that all 10 of Haman's sons were named? It emphasizes their involvement and gives faces to the hate. It's not hard to believe that his sons were filled with the same hate they had witnessed in their father, for this is how most prejudices are cultivated. They were probably leading the charge in Susa on that day. With the death of Haman's sons, God kept his promise to "blot out the memory of Amalek (Deut 25:17-18)." The king asked Esther on that day if there was any other wish he could fulfill for her. She asked for two things: that Haman's sons be hanged on their father's gallows, and for the Jews in Susa to have another day to defend themselves (9:13). Since Haman's influence had been so strong in Susa, Esther wanted to send an equally strong message that the kind of hate-filled prejudice he demonstrated would no longer be tolerated.

Day 26

Victory was won. A wrong was righted. A whole race was rescued from extinction. God had neither forsaken his people nor his covenant with them. The people celebrated as a natural expression of their relief and joy. The party that is described in the rest of chapter 9 was a celebration that continues to this day among the Jewish community. It is called the Feast of Purim. This was such a big deal that the last 13 verses of this chapter outline every detail about the origin of this festival.

Mordecai and Queen Esther heard about all of the celebrations around the provinces, so they decided to make this party an official holiday. The victory of this day needed to be remembered forever. A letter was written and sent out with Mordecai's authority. It declared that every year on the 14th and 15th of Adar, all Jews should have a feast of gladness, send gifts to one another, and give gifts to the poor (9:22).

It was decided that it be called Purim because Haman had callously cast lots (pur) to decide the day of their annihilation. It seems like they could've picked a more positive name, but they chose a negative symbol to commemorate this historical moment. Much like the word "Holocaust" (definition: "destruction or slaughter on a mass scale"), the word "Purim" was chosen to help the Jews remember the story yet never forget the ugliness of hate and prejudice.

A second letter was sent out, perhaps to reiterate the importance of establishing these special days or to give further instructions. Whatever the reason, Queen Esther added her authority to this second letter and the Feast of Purim was "confirmed" and "recorded in writing (9:32)."

The Feast of Purim became one of five important festivals that were observed by the Jewish

> *These three men were used for great good for their own people and even for the nations they served. God sovereignly took them from the much smaller nation of Israel and placed them into influential positions within these powerful empires to accomplish his purposes.*

> *Esther will always represent courage as a willing instrument of God in his sovereign plan to preserve his chosen people and the seed of the promised Messiah.*

community. (You can search the internet for information about this interesting feast). The others are: 1) The Feast of Unleavened bread (Passover); 2) The Feast of Weeks (Pentecost); 3) The Feast of Booths (Tabernacles); 4) The Feast of Lights (Hanukkah).

The Book of Esther ends as it begins—with a statement about the wealth and power of King Ahasuerus. A final description of Mordecai is also given in the short tenth chapter. Much like his predecessors Joseph and Daniel, he was second in rank and power to a pagan king. This never ceases to be amazing when we understand the historical significance of the Egyptian, Babylonian, and Persian empires. These three men were used for great good for their own people and even for the nations they served. God sovereignly took them from the much smaller nation of Israel and placed them into influential positions within these powerful empires to accomplish his purposes.

All we know about Queen Esther and Mordecai is found in this book of the Bible, so let's consider the final words about each of them. Queen Esther leaves the pages of Scripture having put her seal of authority and approval on one of the most celebrated feasts of the Jewish community. Esther will always represent courage as a willing instrument of God in his sovereign plan to preserve his chosen people and the seed of the promised Messiah.

The last two statements made about Mordecai are that he "sought the welfare of his people" and "spoke peace to all his people (10:3)." The New Living Translation puts it like this: "He continued to work for the good of his people and to speak up for the welfare of all their descendants." What a legacy Esther and Mordecai left for their people!

Day 26

Food for Thought
Can the same be said for you? God needs people today who are not afraid to "speak up" for his people, to seek "peace" for our fellow humans, and to seek the welfare of those in need. Obviously, it's easier when it's our family or close friends, but God wants us to see everyone as our "neighbor" and love them (Lk 10:27-37). Who are some "neighbors" that we should be caring for, loving, and speaking up for? What will be the legacy you leave behind when you leave this world?

Faith in Action
Why was the Feast of Purim such a big deal back then? Why does it remain so today? All through the Old Testament, God directed his people to do specific things so that they would not forget important moments. He wanted them to commemorate miraculous events that demonstrated his power, his provision, his protection—who he is and how he works. He even wanted them to remember painful events so that they could reflect on consequences endured, lessons learned, and his faithful love in spite of their unfaithfulness. Read these verses to see how important remembering is to God.

- Deuteronomy 6:1-13
- Deuteronomy 9:6-7
- I Chronicles 16:8-15
- Psalms 78:5-8

We are all prone to forget when something significant happens in our lives—either positive or negative. So, we take pictures or write about it in our journals so that we don't forget. But what happens over time? We forget. Life gets crowded with details and busyness, and significant moments get pushed to the background of our memories. Sometimes when it's unpleasant or painful moments, we even try to make *ourselves forget. The criteria for choosing the things you should remember is to focus on what that event taught you about God, about yourself, and about how God used it in your life to help you grow closer to him.*

- *List some negative consequences for forgetting.*
- *What is the main purpose for remembering?*
- *Should our memories and how we talk about them exalt ourselves or God?*
- *List some events in your life that should be a memorial to you of who God is and what he has done in you and through you.*

Prayer

Sovereign Father, may I continue to trust you with every event in my life, knowing that you will work through all things for my good. May I not forget, even with the most painful moments, how you brought me through injustices, taught me to depend on you when I had no strength, mercifully forgave my unfaithfulness, and continued your work in me through it all. May I always remember and rejoice in the times of your provision, protection, and presence in my life. I praise you and worship you, for you are always good!

Day 27

The Particulars of Providence

Throughout this study, we have talked about God's providence and his sovereignty. We have reiterated that God will always fulfill his purposes, and that his decreed will cannot be thwarted. We have looked up many verses in Scripture that proclaim this truth about God. This has been a recurring theme, because both Ruth and Esther illustrate this so beautifully and clearly. That is why this devotional is named "Portraits of Providence."

A quick search of famous portraits throughout history will reveal a number of classics: American Gothic, Girl with a Pearl Earring, Whistler's Mother, Van Gogh's self portrait, Triple Self Portrait, and of course, the greatest of all time—Mona Lisa. To fully appreciate these portraits, you must have some critical data: the date the painting was created, the period in which it was painted, the medium used, the value of the portrait, and facts or speculations about the person in the portrait. However, the research will reveal the most about the artist. Famous portraits aren't as much about the person being portrayed as they are about the painters who created them. Even though Mona Lisa remains an intriguing woman, the real wonder is the artist, Leonardo Da Vinci.

The same is true about the portraits of our two women—Ruth and Esther. We learned so many interesting things about them as we studied their "portraits" and the important events in their lives. However, the way the "painter's" hand of providence moved across the canvas of history is the real, awe-inspiring story.

Let's pause to make sure that we have a very clear understanding of the providence and sovereignty of God. While these two words are often used interchangeably, their definitions point out some subtle differences. Merriam-Webster notes:

- *Providence* – Divine guidance or care; God conceived as the power sustaining and guiding human destiny.
- *Sovereignty* – Supreme power and rule; freedom from external control; controlling influence.

Let's see how a few theologians define these two words:

- "**Providence** is the means by which God directs all things—both animate and inanimate, seen and unseen, good and evil—toward a worthy purpose, which means His will must finally prevail (J. Vernon McGee from *Edited Messages on Esther*)."
- "God is not just showing up after the trouble and cleaning it up. He is plotting the course and managing the troubles with far-reaching purposes for our good and for the glory of Jesus Christ (John Piper; *A Sweet and Bitter Providence*)."
- "**Sovereignty** is God's control over his creation, dealing with his governance over it: Sovereignty is God's rule over all reality (Norman Geisler; *Systematic Theology*, Vol. 2, 536)."
- "Divine sovereignty is a vast subject: it embraces everything that comes into the biblical picture of God as Lord and King in his world, the One who 'worketh all things after the counsel of his own will (Eph 1:11),' directing every process and ordering every event for the fulfilling of his

Day 27

own eternal plan (J.I. Packer; *Evangelism and the Sovereignty of God*)."

Providence speaks about how God works out his will *in* history. Sovereignty speaks about why he has the authority to decree his will *for* history. Another way to say it is this: *In his sovereignty, God exercises his providential care over his creation to ensure that his divine will is accomplished.*

God's providence was evident in the story of Ruth and Naomi through his loving care for them, his directing of their lives, his protection, and divine provision for them. We saw God's sovereignty displayed in the story of Esther and Mordecai as well. We discovered how God's supreme rule trumped even a most powerful empire's edict. We were able to look behind the curtain and witness how God divinely moved the right pieces into place for his plan to be fulfilled—the preservation of the promised seed and the fulfillment of his covenant.

God's providence is motivated by his supreme love for his creation and his desire to be glorified in everything. God's sovereignty is revealed through his supreme power and rule. God's sovereignty guarantees that his plan for creation will be fulfilled—the redemption and reconciliation of men and women, who can fulfill their kingdom purpose as image-bearers who both worship God and fill the earth with worshipers.

What do the truths of God's providence and sovereignty mean for each of us personally? Questions may flood your mind at this point: Don't I have freedom to choose? Am I just a puppet on God's strings? Can I just sit back, relax, do nothing, and let God do his thing? Isn't it all going to turn out his way in the end anyway? The answers are: Yes! No! No! and Yes! Wait a minute. These answers seem incongruous. Let's do what we should always do when things

> *In his sovereignty, God exercises his providential care over his creation to ensure that his divine will is accomplished.*

> *God's providence is motivated by his supreme love for his creation and his desire to be glorified in everything. God's sovereignty is revealed through his supreme power and rule.*

get confusing—let's review what we know to be true.

First, God reveals everything he wants us to know about himself through his word and his Son. We can learn so many things about him, and we can even know him personally, but we cannot know him completely. He is incomprehensible, which means we will never be able to understand him wholly. He is simply too big (Ps 145:3; Rom 11:33)! So, don't be discouraged or full of doubt when you bump up against a truth about God that you just can't get your mind around. That's supposed to happen.

Instead, we should bow to his supremacy. We should humble ourselves and acknowledge that there will always be more to learn about our great God. And, we should trust him with the mysteries of his infinite greatness. Be encouraged that this is the God who is working for you, in you, and through you to accomplish his divine purposes.

Second, God has revealed the way that he wants us to live. Jesus exemplified that type of obedient life. In Christ, we have the freedom to choose to follow Christ's example, obey his commands, and strive to please him with our worship and obedience. This choice should be an outworking of our love and appreciation for his constant grace and mercy toward us.

Third, we should find comfort in the fact that even our propensity for disobedience cannot derail God's good purposes for us. The fact that we will be held responsible for our disobedience, however, can motivate us to surrender to his authority in our lives. Daily, we should choose to be willing vessels (like Ruth and Esther),

> *Don't be discouraged or full of doubt when you bump up against a truth about God that you just can't get your mind around. That's supposed to happen.*

Day 27

allowing God to make us blessed participants in his kingdom work in the world. He may not need us to accomplish his plan, but he delights in using broken and willing vessels to accomplish his work—this is the way that he is glorified (2 Cor 4:7).

Together, we have seen that God was sovereignly moving through these fascinating events—small and great—to fulfill his divine purposes. That same God is providentially working in your life, too. Never forget that God is amazing, powerful, and worthy of our most devoted worship and allegiance.

Food for Thought *Living in the reality of God's sovereignty can fill us with peace for the present instead of fear for the future. God has it all under control. In fact, nothing is outside of his control, and nothing is without purpose. This should abolish anxiety and worry from your life. Resting in his loving providence and purposeful sovereignty will allow you to face every circumstance with confidence that God is working all things for his glory and for your good.*

Faith in Action *Are you struggling with worry or anxiety? Are you so busy trying to control your circumstances or to fix your problems that you are forgetting to look to the one who is in control? If so, these are the areas of your life where you need to submit to God's sovereign rule. Go ahead—name these areas and write them down on a piece of paper. Your willingness to acknowledge them can be the first step to peace. As a demonstration of your surrender, pick the paper up and then symbolically lay it down somewhere as you pray the prayer below.*

Prayer *Thank you, God, for your loving providence in my life. I worship you and submit to you as my gracious, sovereign ruler. Today, I lay down my worries and anxieties and put them into your hands. I want to live in peace and confidence that nothing is outside of your control. Even when the worst seems to be happening, help me to trust that you are my sovereign Father, and you are working all things for my good and for your divine purposes.*

Vessels of Providence

Think of five women in the Bible that are main characters or have significant roles. Which woman do you think would be the "most worthy" to have a book of the Bible named after her? Did you think of Eve—the original woman and mother of humanity? What about Sarah or Rebekah or Miriam or Deborah? Maybe Esther, but certainly not Ruth. Of course, Mary, the mother of Jesus, would top our list. She's a "main" character and most definitely "significant." Yet, Ruth and Esther were chosen for this honor. Pretty cool, huh? Let's take one last look at our two, leading ladies.

Ruth was like every average, blue-collar woman. She was not a superstar by any means. She had no special talents and no important family name—just a beautiful, servant's heart. God did not put her on center stage like he did Esther. She simply lived, loved, gave, served, and committed her life to following Naomi's God in the small Jewish community of Bethlehem. He saved her from a life of pagan idolatry to become a God-fearer. She was plucked from anonymity and placed into the ancestry of the promised Messiah. As a Gentile, Ruth is a beautiful illustration of how God desires to redeem and reclaim ALL people, not just his chosen people Israel. No one is exempt from the chance to receive God's grace, mercy, and forgiveness.

> As a Gentile, Ruth is a beautiful illustration of how God desires to redeem and reclaim ALL people, not just his chosen people Israel.

Esther was a female counterpart to Daniel. Both were young, Jewish exiles, sovereignly chosen for influential positions in pagan empires. However, the contrasts between the two show us that God is not bound by specific methods or means. Daniel was captured at the beginning of the Babylonian captivity and placed into the "Babylon School for the Gifted." He stood out among his peers as well, but in very different ways. His courage and boldness stood out from the very beginning. He wore his faith and his ethnicity loud and proud. He was so courageous with his faith, that he was unconcerned about his life and ended up in the lions' den because of it. He was not subtly trying to fit in so that he didn't offend anyone. His faith was rock solid, and courage was not a problem for him.

Esther, on the other hand, was different. She was taken against her will and did everything she was asked, even those things that went against her faith traditions. She stood out among her peers, not for her bold declarations, but because of her humility and gracious spirit. She hid her ethnicity, and when Mordecai asked for her help, she was terribly afraid of losing her life. Obviously, her faith was not as strong as Daniel's. She lacked courage and had to implore God to provide it for her. Esther is proof that God can take paralyzing fear and turn it into courageous obedience. Despite their different personalities, God used them both. Isn't that encouraging?

> Esther is proof that God can take paralyzing fear and turn it into courageous obedience.

The Book of Esther is a history lesson about how God preserved his promised seed at a crucial time when the nation of Israel faced mass genocide. He used the fledgling courage of a young queen to turn the tables on a wicked

Day 28

scheme against his people. Unlike Ruth, Esther did become a superstar of sorts among her people—another example of the different ways God accomplishes his plans.

What a great reminder that God uses all kinds of people in many different ways. He is not about cookie-cutter models or means. Naomi and Mordecai were also very different people, but God used them for his purposes.

> *Every member of the family of God is important and has value by virtue of the fact that we are his workmanship. God doesn't need us to accomplish his kingdom purposes, but he delights to use us—all of us.*

In fact, neither Ruth nor Esther's stories would be possible or complete without Naomi and Mordecai's stories. Every member of the family of God is important and has value by virtue of the fact that "we are his workmanship (Eph 2:10)." Like we said yesterday, God doesn't need us to accomplish his kingdom purposes, but he delights to use us—all of us. The only requirement is to be willing and obedient vessels—like Ruth and Esther.

Food for Thought You may be feeling unworthy or incapable of being used by God. You may feel that you lack the necessary qualities for God to use you. Let's not forget that Ruth, Naomi, Esther, and Mordecai demonstrated qualities that each of us can employ with God's help—kindness, a diligent work ethic, selflessness, humility, teachability, courage, and a willingness to look to God for help, just to name a few. Which of these qualities do you need to ask God to build in your life?

Faith in Action A vessel is simply a hollow container. A hollow container is meant to be used. It can be used for good or bad depending on its contents. A simple Mason jar or a priceless Ming-Dynasty vase can hold a life-giving drink of water for a dying man—he could care less about its value. It's not about how the container looks on the outside. The only thing that matters is the availability of the vessel and what's put in it. Read the following and answer the questions:

- Romans 6:12-14 – For what purposes can the "instruments" (i.e. vessels) in these verses be used? What are the two directives that will ensure that your body will be used as an "instrument" for righteousness?

- Philippians 1:9-11 – With what are we to be filled? How does that happen?

- Ephesians 3:14-21 – How can we be filled with "all the fullness of God" according to these verses? What can God accomplish when we are filled like that?

Day 28

Prayer — Dear Father in heaven, forgive me for obeying the passions of my sinful desires. Here and now I offer myself to you as a willing vessel to be used. Cleanse me so that I can be filled with the fruit of righteousness and used for your kingdom purposes. I am so humbled and grateful that you desire to use me. I can't wait to be a part of what you are doing in your kingdom. It is far more abundantly than all I can ask or think. Your power is at work in me—Wow! Make me your willing, faithful, and obedient vessel.

Day 29

Comfort or Courage?

Let's do something fun—give the first answer that comes to your mind. Casual stroll or steep mountain climb? Speed boat or river cruise? Ride in first class or tandem sky diving? Race car or limousine? Roller coaster or merry-go-round? Movie night in or escape-room outing? Stay on the path or get as close to the edge as possible? Same seat every Sunday or different seat each week? Have a plan or play it by ear?

Your answers reveal whether you are naturally inclined to security or danger; routine or adventure; taking risks or playing it safe; comfort or courage. Everyone's personality is different. Neither one is right or wrong—at least in these examples. But when it comes to the kingdom of God, comfort can be our enemy. It can hold us back from experiencing all that God desires to do in us and through us.

Our two special women provide a wonderful example for us when it comes to living life beyond our comfort zones. Ruth was willing to leave the security of the familiar to follow Naomi to a new family, a new faith, and a new future. If she had been afraid to venture out of her comfort zone, she would never have put feet to her faith and left Moab.

She didn't hide in her safe little house in Bethlehem, either. She was unselfishly courageous, willing to go

> *When it comes to the kingdom of God, comfort can be our enemy.*

out on her own to seek provision for Naomi and herself in a community where she was an outsider. She was willing to work harder than she had ever worked. She embraced change and didn't cower in the face of difficulty.

Esther was not really given a choice in her life-changing circumstance, but once she was in it, she graciously adapted to her forced captivity. She didn't rebel against her unusual and undesirable circumstances when all of her choices were taken away from her. She didn't spend her time sulking in self-pity; instead, she made the best of her situation. She didn't cower when faced with the terrifying risk of going before the king uninvited. Rather, Esther entrusted herself to God and surrendered to his purposes.

God routinely calls people to courageous action, outside their comfort zones. There's a good reason for that. When impossible things are accomplished by broken, fallible human beings, God gets the glory! That's how the world takes notice that there is a God in heaven who is worth knowing and worshiping. And, that is what God has been after all along.

God called Abram to leave the home he knew for a place he didn't know—one that God would show him on the journey (Gen 12:1-3). Because of Abram's courageous obedience, God would make him the father of a great new nation, which would produce the Savior of the world. God called Moses to leave his safe, hiding place in the desert to go back into Egypt to deliver his people from slavery (Ex 3:1-10). Although Moses had to fight his cowardice, he obeyed and became one of the only humans to meet with God "face to face (Ex 33:11, 17-23)." God asked

> *God routinely calls people to courageous action, outside their comfort zones.*

Day 29

Joshua (Joshua 6) and Gideon (Judges 7) to engage in unconventional warfare to display his glory. Think of the courage and trust it took for them to follow God's unusual battle strategies. God called David from his tranquil, sheep pasture (1 Sam 16) into the hotbed of political intrigue. Even though David's life was in jeopardy for much of the time, he courageously walked into God's sovereign plan for his life. God asked Paul to lay aside his honored, Jewish pedigree and follow him into a life of service and suffering (Phil 3:4-8). As a result, Paul is considered the greatest missionary this world has ever known.

> *When impossible things are accomplished by broken, fallible human beings, God gets the glory!*

There are many other examples from Scripture, but you get the message. Comfort zones are not God's thing. They may be comfortable for us, because we get to feel like we're in control. But, we don't need to live with courage or trust in God in our comfort zone. Truth be told, we don't even need God. That kind of living is powerless, joyless, and dishonoring to God.

Yes, our sinful nature tempts us to stay in our comfortable bubble; to reject God's call to expand our boundaries and to get involved in a God-sized mission. Our desire for familiar, faith-routines can cause us to be short-sighted and spiritually lazy. We can get so self-absorbed in our own faith communities that we don't even notice a world that desperately needs Jesus. We can be so scared of offending someone that we never risk sharing the truth of the gospel—the only solution to this world's problems.

> *Our desire for familiar, faith-routines can cause us to be short-sighted and spiritually lazy.*

Let's face it. It takes courage to step out and risk rejection or ridicule. A disciple's life of following Christ will be uncomfortable, risky, dangerous, or even painful. Ask Paul. In 2 Corinthians 11:23-28, he gave a long, descriptive list of the challenges of following Christ. Yet, in Philippians, Paul declared that every loss he had experienced paled in comparison to "the surpassing worth of knowing Christ Jesus (3:8)." Courageous obedience leads to a life of countless joys (Rom 15:13; 1 Pet 1:8-9) and eternal rewards (2 Cor 4:17-18; James 1:12).

Day 29

Food for Thought We read Ephesians 3:14-21 yesterday in our Faith in Action exercise. Read it again. In these verses, we see faith with roots (3:17) and faith with wings (3:20). However, the words "rooted and grounded" do not mean comfort and safety. Instead, it is about being so grounded in Christ's love for us, and our love for him, that we are filled with God's fullness. This fullness gives us all that we need: knowledge, strength, and the Holy Spirit's power. These are strong roots (3:16). Then, we are in a place where we can soar with God as he does amazing things beyond anything we can imagine (3:20).

Faith in Action What comforts and routines are you resting in or holding onto today? What makes you afraid? What is holding you back from complete surrender and a willingness to follow Christ into "more . . . than all that [you] can ask or think (Eph 3:20)?" Go ahead, make a list. It helps to name it and see your answers in black and white. God is wanting to use you, but it takes effort on your part.

Read 2 Peter 1:3-11.

- List the things that God has already done for you as a child of God. What are some incredible gifts that God has given you by virtue of who you are in Christ?

- Now list some things you are called to do in these verses. What efforts are you to make? What are the words that speak to actions you should take?

God has given you everything you need. Now quit being a spiritual couch-potato. Make that first courageous move away from your comfy spot and see what adventure God has for you today!

Prayer

Dear God, I thank you that you are the all-powerful one! I am amazed that your divine power has given me everything that I need to live the life that you desire for me. I don't want to stay in my comfort zones and become "ineffective or unfruitful." Give me courage to follow you wherever you want to take me.

Day 30

Life-Changing Encounters

We have reached the end of our journey through *30-Days to Ruth and Esther: Portraits of Providence*. We have traveled together from the pagan streets of Moab to the little town of Bethlehem then wandered east to the winter capital of the Persian empire, Susa. Who could help but notice the contrasts of the humble cottage of Naomi and Ruth to the opulent furnishings of Esther's dwelling; the swaying barley fields to the manicured gardens of the Persian palace; the servant leadership of Boaz to the selfishness and narcissism of King Ahasuerus. Through all the different characters, scenes, and events, the sovereign hand of God's providence has been the connecting thread.

Every time you open God's word to study it, there is great potential for a life-changing encounter. This potential is realized when you read God's word with purposeful intent, an open mind, and a surrendered heart. Here are a few questions to ask that can help you when you read any passage of Scripture:

Through all the different characters, scenes, and events, the sovereign hand of God's providence has been the connecting thread.

- What does this text teach me about who God is and how he works?

Every time you open God's word to study it, there is great potential for a life-changing encounter.

- What does this text show me about mankind—our sinfulness and how we respond to God?

- What does this text teach me about Jesus? Do I see a shadow of him in the story?

- Where do I see the gospel in this text (i.e. redemptive pictures or illustrations)?

- How does God want to use the truths I learned in this text to transform my life?

Let me help you answer a couple of these questions, and then you can answer the rest on the next page. Let's look at the places where we can see Jesus and the gospel in our two books. In the Book of Ruth, we have already talked about Boaz—the kinsman redeemer—a portrait of Christ (if necessary, look back at Day 8 to refresh your memory). When Ruth asked Boaz to spread his "wings" over her (3:9), this prefigured Christ spreading his loving protection over his bride, the church (Eph 5:25-27). Of course, one of the main messages in Ruth is that Gentiles would be included in God's covenant promise of salvation (Gal 3:7-9, 29). Ruth is a beautiful example of a pagan, Gentile woman placing her faith in the God of Israel and committing her life to follow him. The message of the gospel is clear that Christ's offer of redemption is extended to everyone who will receive it.

In the Book of Esther, we see God bringing deliverance to his people, which is a preview of Christ delivering us from the power of sin through his death and resurrection. Esther's willingness to die for her people prefigures Christ's willingness to sacrifice himself for sinful mankind. Like Joseph, Mordecai also gives us a picture of Christ as the rescuer of his people from destruction.

Day 30

> *One of the main messages in Ruth is that Gentiles would be included in God's covenant promise of salvation*

We sometimes make the mistake of thinking that the gospel is only told in the New Testament. But, these are powerful, gospel pictures, and they are right in the middle of the Old Testament. The silhouette of Christ is seen in the first Messianic prophecy of Genesis 3:15. Then, with each new covenant that God makes with man (i.e. Abrahamic, Davidic, etc.), the details of the promised seed become clearer and clearer. By the time Jesus was born in Bethlehem, he had been prophesied and prefigured so frequently that those who earnestly seek him have no trouble recognizing him for who he is—"A light for revelation to the Gentiles, and for glory to your people Israel (Lk 2:25-32)."

Hebrews 4:12 says, "For the word of God is living and active, sharper than any two-edged sword, piercing to the division of soul and of spirit, of joints and of marrow, and discerning the thoughts and intentions of the heart." This is the powerful word that can produce life change. The word of God is alive and can cut away our masks and tear down our walls; it can pierce to the very place in our heart that needs attention, even those places that we think we have hidden from everyone. Where did the sword of God's word pierce your heart with knowledge, conviction, or encouragement over the last 30 days? As you spend the next few minutes with God concluding this study, answer a few of the questions we mentioned earlier.

> *The word of God is alive and can cut away our masks and tear down our walls; it can pierce to the very place in our heart that needs attention, even those places that we think we have hidden from everyone.*

1. What have you learned or been reminded about God through this study?

2. What were some interesting things that stood out to you about how God works?

3. What character from either book was the most fascinating to you? Why?

4. Did you learn anything from any of the characters—positively or negatively? Could you relate to any of them?

5. List some things that encouraged you in your walk with God through this study.

6. List some things that convicted you.

7. What prompted you to seek God for transformation?

It is my hope that you've had some life-changing encounters over the past 30 days—not only with our characters but also with the God who "works all things according to the counsel of his will (Eph 1:11)." As you've opened God's word day after day, my prayer is two-fold:

- I pray that the truths you have encountered during these 30 days will never leave you and will forever change you.

- I pray that you will always continue to grow in your knowledge of our loving, sovereign Father and his son, Jesus Christ, our redeemer. Keep studying God's word and never stop!

Finding L.I.F.E. in Jesus!

Everyone wants to be happy. The hard part is determining exactly what that means. For some, happiness is defined through relationships. They believe that popularity, a huge friend list on Facebook, and a significant other produces happiness. For others, happiness is defined through success. They believe that personal achievement, a huge number in their bank account, and plenty of expensive toys produces happiness. For still others, happiness is defined through community. They believe that personal growth, a huge impact for societal change, and embracing diversity produces happiness. And these things do—until they don't.

Experiencing happiness is as difficult as catching the greased pig at the county fair. It appears to be right in front of us, but then it slips through our fingers and is gone. Friends, achievement, and personal growth have the potential to bring happiness into our lives, but when our friends disappear, success eludes us, and we realize that we're incapable of self–transformation, happiness is quickly replaced by disillusionment and depression. The problem with pursuing happiness is that it is an emotion that is driven by our circumstances. And let's be honest—we all tend to have more negative than positive experiences in our lives.

So, what's the answer? Should we keep doing the same things while expecting different results, or should we consider what Jesus has to say about finding our purpose for life? If you want to stay on the hamster wheel while you try to catch up to happiness, you can stop reading here. But if you're ready to consider what God wants to do in your life, please read on.

God never promises happiness in the Bible. Are you surprised to hear that? Instead, he promises something much greater—joy. While happiness is an emotion fueled by circumstance, joy is an attitude fueled by God's Spirit. Happiness is self–determined. In other words, I am the sole determiner of whether I'm happy at any given moment. Joy, on the other hand, is God–determined. God has promised to give us joy, and it isn't based on our circumstances—it's based on God's character and promises.

This is why Jesus never talks about giving people happiness. He knew all too well that chasing happiness is like chasing your shadow. You can never catch it. Instead, he talks about giving people life. He said, "I came that they may have life and have it abundantly (Jn 10:10)." Here, Jesus reveals that the thing people really want, whether they know it or not, is abundant life. To have an abundant life means that you are personally satisfied in all areas of your life, and you experience peace and contentment as a result. Jesus' statement also means that we do not have the capacity to create that kind of life for ourselves. Jesus came in order to give it to us. But how? The Bible tells us that achieving this kind of satisfied life requires us to know something about God, ourselves, and the reason for the death and resurrection of Jesus Christ.

First, we must understand God's **love**. The Bible says that God is love (I Jn 4:8), and God created us so that we could know him and experience his love (Gen 1:26–31). God created us to be worshipers and to live forever in the reality of his glory. And, when sin marred his perfect creation, he created a plan to free men and women from its curse. At just the right time in history, God sent his own Son, Jesus, into our world. "For God so loved the

Finding L.I.F.E. in Jesus!

world, that he gave his only Son, that whoever believes in him should not perish but have eternal life (Jn 3:16)." It is God's love that motivates him to restore relationship with those who are separated from him by sin.

Second, we must understand our **isolation**. To be isolated is to be separated from someone, and as a result, to be alone. This is what sin has done to us. It has separated us from the very one we were created to know, love, and worship—God. When Adam and Eve rebelled against God by breaking the lone command he had given them, the entire world was brought under the curse of sin (Gen 3). As a result, God removed them from the Garden of Eden, and their perfect fellowship with God was broken. In an instant, they had become isolated from God because of their sin. From that moment to this, every person born into this world is guilty of sin. The Bible says, "For all have sinned and fall short of the glory of God (Rom 3:23)." Because of this "there is none righteous, no, not one (Rom 3:10)." Further, "The wages of sin is death (Rom 6:23a)." We were created to love and worship God in perfect community, but now because of sin we are isolated from him. Meanwhile, we try to satisfy this desire to know God by pursuing our own happiness, even though we can never hope to attain it. And in doing so, we risk being isolated from God for all eternity.

Third, we must understand our need for **forgiveness.** There is only one way to experience God's love and escape the isolation caused by sin—we must experience God's forgiveness. In spite of sin, God never stopped loving the people he created. He promised Adam and Eve that he would send someone who could fix the problem they had created. When it was time, God sent his own Son, Jesus, to be the world's Savior. This, too, was an act of God's love. The Bible says, "God shows his love for us in that while we were still sinners, Christ died for us (Rom 5:8)." When Jesus died on the cross, he was paying the penalty for our sins (Rom 3:23–26). When God raised Jesus from the dead, it was to demonstrate that forgiveness was available to all who would receive it by faith. Paul explained how this happens in his letter to the Ephesians. "For by grace you have been saved through faith. And this is not your own doing; it is the gift of God, not a result of works, so that no one may boast (Eph 2:8–9)."

The reality is that we cannot experience salvation as a result of our own efforts. We can try to be a good person, go to a church, even give a ton of money to worthy causes—none of these "works" can provide forgiveness. No matter how hard we try, we will always "fall short of the glory of God." That is why we must receive God's offer of forgiveness and salvation by faith. Faith simply means to trust or believe. Salvation requires us to believe that God loves us, that we are isolated from him by our sins, and that his Son Jesus died and was raised to life again to pay the sin debt that we owe God because of our sins. When we take God up on his offer of the gift of salvation, he doesn't just give us forgiveness—he gives us life! The Bible says, "The free gift of God is eternal life in Christ Jesus our Lord (Rom 6:23)."

Fourth, we must understand the **enjoyment** that comes from knowing, loving, and worshiping God. Whether we know it or not, we are slaves to sin until God sets us free (Rom 6:20–23). This was the ultimate reason that God sent his Son, Jesus, to die on the cross for our sins—God sent Jesus so that we could be set free from our sins. Jesus said, "You will know the truth, and the truth will set you free. . . . Everyone who commits sin is a slave to sin. . . . So, if the Son sets you free, you will be free indeed (Jn 8:32–36)." Jesus was teaching us that we must be set free from sin in order to enjoy the life that God has given us—both now and in eternity future. We are set free when we commit our lives to Jesus Christ through faith in his death and resurrection. Then, and only then, will we find joy in the abundant life of Jesus Christ!

So, the question for you is a simple one: Are you ready to experience freedom from sin and the abundant life that Jesus promised you? If so, God is waiting for you to talk with him about it (Jer 29:13). Stop right where you are and make this your prayer to God:

Finding L.I.F.E. in Jesus!

"Father in heaven, I know that I'm a sinner. I know that I've done lots of things that displease you and disappoint you. And, I know that I'm isolated from you because of my sin. I know that if I die without knowing you, I will spend forever separated from you in hell. But, I believe that Jesus is your sinless Son, and I believe that he died on the cross for me. I believe that he died to provide a perfect payment for my sin debt. I believe that you raised him from the dead so that I could experience forgiveness for my sins. Right now, Father, I'm asking you to forgive me of my sins and save me. I am receiving your Son Jesus as my personal Lord and Savior. I will follow you the rest of my life. Please give me the joy of a life spent knowing, loving, and worshiping you. I ask these things in Jesus' name, Amen."

If you made the decision to accept Jesus as your Savior today, we want to talk with you! Please contact the people at www.seed–publishing–group.com. We would love to talk with you about your decision and help you with your first steps in following Jesus!

If you enjoyed *30 Days to Ruth/Esther*, check out the other books in the *30 Days to the Bible* series.

Also from Seed Publishing:

Made in the USA
Columbia, SC
24 July 2021